PENTECOSTALISM

AND

IMMIGRATION

DAVID DOUGLAS

Edited by Sheila Douglas

IMCGB Publications

DEDICATION

This book is dedicated to all those

who have encouraged and supported IMCGB in the past

all who support and work for IMCGB at the present time

and all who will carry forward the Vision of the Council in the future,

to the glory of God.

Opposite is a portrait of the late David Douglas,
Founder and Moderator of IMCGB,
The Second Pentecostal Archbishop,
and author of this record of IMCGB's beginnings and philosophy.
Drawn in 1973 by Margaret Lewis

Copyright © 2008   IMCGB Publications

ISBN 978 1 871757 002

Formatted and Produced by DX Imaging
    Unit 20, 25 Greenhill Crescent, Watford WD18 8EA.
    T 01923 227644, F 01923 816 896, www.dxgraphics.co.uk

Acknowledgements

The editor wishes to thank the following for the assistance they have given:

IMCGB Secretary General, Rt. Rev. Onye Obika, for support and encouragement and tireless effort to establish the Vision of the Council, the IMCGB.

IMCGB Publications Committee, especially the Chief Editor, Rev. I. Owoyemi, and Rev. G. Sarfo-Duah for critical reading of the manuscript.

Rev. Emily Obika for constant encouragement.

Churches Together in Britain and Ireland for permission to quote *The Swanwick Declaration*, which is Chapter 3 of *Churches Together in Pilgrimage*, published in 1989 by British Council of Churches. *The Swanwick Declaration* is Appendix 1, see page 142.

NB   Quotations from scripture are from the following versions: Authorised Version (AV), New International Version (NIV), New Living Translation (NLT).

   IMCGB is a registered charity, number 269440

CONTENTS

Introduction VIII

Chapter 1	**Strangers**	**1**
Chapter 2	**Action**	**29**
Chapter 3	**In the Public Eye**	**43**
Chapter 4	**Working Together**	**62**
Chapter 5	**Grass Roots and Government**	**75**
Chapter 6	**Making a Way forward**	**95**
Chapter 7	**A Look at Pentecostalism**	**113**
Chapter 8	**No Longer Strangers but Pilgrims Together**	**133**
Appendix 1	Swanwick Declaration	142
Appendix 2	Extract from address to Nigerian Churches	145
Appendix 3	The Future	147
Appendix 4	What is IMCGB? How to join IMCGB	149
Appendix 5	IMCGB Recognised Colleges	151
Appendix 6	IMCGB Management Diagram	153
Appendix 7	IMCGB Personnel	155
Appendix 8	Basis and Commitment of CTE	157
Editor's Note		158

INTRODUCTION

This book is written to express, both in practice and in theory, the life of true Pentecostalism, based upon the common daily life of Jesus first, working with his father in his carpenter trade, and the call of Andrew, Peter, James and John from their personal common occupation as fishermen, and Matthew from a different rank as the tax collector.

Jesus linked up each man as he went along, calling them from various backgrounds, making himself an example to them, as well as to John the Baptist, a wild man living off locusts and wild honey, in description a primitive type of man. Yet Jesus was able to show the superior power in practice, when he was able to call them and they followed, to tell them and they obeyed, but never did he practice too much mysticism, except when he spoke of the Kingdom of Heaven to come hereafter.

That seems mysterious, but they understood, because Jesus was able to live out a simple life like them, and make that life be worthwhile, in doing a miracle when it was necessary to do so, and in doing a day's work the ordinary way, when it was necessary to do so, to discuss and face problems and trials and temptations like any human being, yet have the dimension of his powers, the miracle-working, mysterious power. He only occasionally used a small amount of that power to demonstrate that there is such a power.

The work my colleagues and I have done, long and hard and slow though it seemed, was done because it is the life and acts of Jesus Christ and the Apostles. Jesus is the Cornerstone upon which we must build as testimony to the Faith we are commanded to live, teach and preach. This is a phenomenon of intrinsic worth requiring no further supporting argument. It has to be done.

David Douglas, April 1992.

CHAPTER ONE

Strangers

"The burden which Habakkuk, the prophet, did see."

The Holy Bible (AV), Habakkuk 1:1

OUT OF SLAVERY
FAITH IN YOUTH
A MIND OF PRAYER

ALONE AND IN THE DARK
SMALL BEGINNINGS
ESTABLISHING

FACTIONS AND ELEMENTS
NEW THOUGHTS AND A WAY AHEAD

PREPARATIONS
IN THE LOCAL TOWN 1967
TOWARDS NATIONAL CHURCH LINKS
LOCAL CONSULTATIONS
SORROWS

"Hallelujah!" he cried, tears running down his face. *"We have crossed the Red Sea. We are on our way to the Promised Land!" It was clear that the simple ceremony that had just taken place was of far greater importance than a casual onlooker would be able to understand. A relatively small group of Ministers, Pastors and Leaders of Black Pentecostal Churches had honoured four of their colleagues on account of their distinctive and widely recognised work in Britain. As medallions were presented and tears flowed, I, who had worked towards this goal for twenty years, joined in the hymns of joy.**

*See pp102-103.

OUT OF SLAVERY

I was born in St. Anns, Jamaica, on 8th June 1934, the tenth of eleven children, eight boys and three girls.

Mother and Father, professional farmers, had built and ran a Baptist Church and school. They later employed the first Head Teacher, J. A. Joe, and the first Parson there, Parson Johnson.

These two professionals were the first to be involved in our community after the relaxation of the slave trade, when people moved away from the slave stations to seek land for farming and family settlements. That period was about 1910 to 1915.

Life was hard. You had to walk four or five miles to school and back, morning and evening, sometimes in the pouring rain, with mud up to your waist, only to spend hours in those wet clothes! In drought you had to walk on tough, dry clay that bruised your toes and blistered the soles of your feet.

When you got home you had to help with the animals: feed pigs, chickens, cows, horses, goats, mules, donkeys; and help gather in the produce: cane, oranges, ginger, coffee, cocoa and the rest.

Then, of course, study and homework!! When would it all end?

But there was always a consolation to look forward to. We would all meet together – yes sir! Even the dogs in our family had to go to prayer meetings every night and early every morning. I remember the songs we would sing, such as, "When I kneel to pray," "Kneel at the Cross," "Draw me, Saviour, Draw me," "My Jesus, I love Thee," and "Blessed hour of prayer."

My Mother was a very good singer, so was Daddy, and how everyone would join in singing Psalms, saying proverbs and having Bible studies! Blessings were said by Father and Mother. They always asked God to shield us from dangers, for many dangers faced us because of the difficult things we had to do in those hard conditions. God surely did shield us and our parents. All eleven of us lived to grow up, marry and have children.

FAITH IN YOUTH

All who receive good blessings have to be tested, the great and the small, the established and the beginner. From time to time, Mother and Father took produce to market, while older children were at school and other people concentrated on things they must do before Mum and Dad came back. This was a day when my sister Monica and I were going to die! Until now I am convinced that we did die. I know I am alive and so is she, because I am telling you what took place. I was six years old and she was four. Why were we dying?

Bitter Cassava is widely used for various kinds of food, starch and baby food. It is widely cultivated in Afro-Caribbean and Asian countries, but it must be grated or milled and all the starch and then all the water taken out. The food is then milled again to flour before it is safe to eat. Some people, however, after removing the starch, use a towel to squeeze out the water, and bake the head (as they call it) with sugar and spices. They call it bammy. It's a bit like chappati.

Cassava water is a deadly poison. Cows, horses, donkeys, chickens and birds have died in seconds from it. If it gets within reach of animals they are sure to drink it and there will be no time for recovery. It will be instant death. Monica and I got our towels that day, squeezed as we had seen others do to get the water out, but without their strength and skill. Worse still, we did not know how long it should be baked in the sauce pot until it was dried out and became clammy and brown. So we did it our way and shared the one we had made.

As we swallowed the first mouthful I felt a dreadful pain in my belly and Monica screamed and threw herself to the ground. Our bellies began to swell at such a rate that we could see them stretching as we gasped for breath. I said to my sister, "We are poisoned by the cassava." She said, "Are we dying?" "Yes!" I said. Then we started saying "Lord save us! Lord don't let us die! Lord wait till Mummy and Daddy and our brothers are here! Lord help!"

Then I remembered that my father always kept red soil and a nut called busy. If people or animals are poisoned and you can get them to eat this mixture quickly enough you could slow down the rapid rate of the poison going through the body.

We ate some of this stuff, and although we were still very ill we were not dying as fast as before. A relation, passing from the cane field, heard us screaming and rushed in. As he saw our bellies and the sauce pot he screamed, "Lord Gad! De baby dem poison!" He picked up both of us, ran outside and spread the news with a loud, echoing voice. The whole district came running. Some were praying. Some were comforting. Some were giving us all sorts of antedotes.

They sent horseriders galloping to fetch our parents who were some ten miles away. They came back with Dr. Mullard, but when he came he said the danger had been averted, adding that it was more than a miracle. When this assurance was given loud cries of "Praise the Lord" came from the people of the district and my relations.

My sister and I had experienced our first miracle of God's love and mercy through prayer, action and faith.

A MIND OF PRAYER

Further testing of faith was to come. My eldest sister and Mother's chief helper, Katherine, had to leave to begin her new married life a hundred miles away. Within a few months Mother suddenly became ill with a total collapse of her nervous system that almost crippled all Daddy's business since he had to stay at home to look after her. Mother had to be nursed night and day and that was to be so for three years. It was seven years before she was completely back to normal again. Monica and I were sent to stay with Katherine at Montego Bay. Katherine had to travel backwards and forwards because she also had her husband and his business to attend to. Daddy worked and prayed, nursed Mummy and prayed. Mummy, even lying on her back unable to turn, still was able to pray for others who came to see her just to receive the touch of her hands. Then they felt better and that gave her more faith to struggle to overcome a very destructive disease. My mother recovered and eventually died at the age of 96 in November 1986. At my mother's funeral there were Christians from all parts of the world, to pay their respects to one of the most faithful and prayerful persons who lived within Victorian times.

As I grew up I learnt to live with a special faith, developing a mind of prayer within my heart. I never asked for anything for myself, except that if I felt I had done anything wrong I asked for forgiveness. I was constantly praying for others. That became a way of life, especially from the day my sister and I were dying.

I came to realise that I belonged to a special family who lived by faith and that the grace and gifts of God were present in our lives. I was baptised when I was 15, and at 16 entered college to study for the Ministry. I had built up a large caseload of clientele. There were people asking me to visit them, people coming to where I lived to see me specially for prayer. People who could have been my parents, if they had a family problem, depression, were going through a bad patch or were sick, would send for me to talk to them or pray for them. Also I was able to select herbs and bushes both to drink as medicine or to use externally, to cure people of rheumatism, gall bladder trouble, lumbago and such things. I had a special way with animals as well. Animals who had become aggressive were completely calm and subdued when they came into my handling.

ALONE AND IN THE DARK

I came to England in 1958 but life here was not quite what I had expected. Not one of my four brothers and my sister and their families were going to Church. They told me that the Churches were not welcoming to black people.

So we turned to prayer in our own hearts and Church Service in our own souls and God then became to me very private. As the months passed I became sad, lonely and depressed. I used to pray and cry as I walked through the local park to and from work in the mornings and evenings. I did not cry in the house, because my brothers and other members of their families would have found out my plight and become too worried. Everyone here and at home in Jamaica would have been very sad.

The less committed Christians from various parts of the world did not miss out as much as my family. We were used to Sunday Service and Sunday night meeting, and on weekdays Evening Services, Prayer Meetings, visits, meeting one another, looking after the sick and praying for them to be healed, and standing by those who were in trouble through no fault of their own to give them support and love, hoping that one day they would give their support to the work as we gave ours.

Other newcomers to England experienced a different kind of frustration as they sought friendship and pleasure in public houses, night clubs, various societies and recreational contexts. They realised that they were not welcome. They were rebuffed and forced to resort to home-based activities: house parties, loud music and excessive alcohol drinking that later developed into drug addiction. This led to the distant relationship between police and immigrant communities, making law and order and race relations become more difficult as more and more immigrants came to Britain. 1962 was the peak year.

These issues presented us with Church and community problems as strangers in a strange land.

SMALL BEGINNINGS

In late summer 1958 one of my elder brothers, Ken, joined us in England from Bermuda. My youngest sister, Monica, also came. I thought, "Thank God! Together we will encourage each other, make a go of it and find some happiness." There were now five brothers here: Oscar, Ken, Leo, Harry and myself, and two sisters: Dorothy and Monica. We would, by God's grace, make a contribution to help these islands become more conscious of Christian awakening and a more acceptable place for strangers, some of whom were to become citizens and permanent residents.

A few weeks after Ken and Monica arrived we started to pray together. We began to go to Putney to visit and pray with Dorothy, to George and family in Hayes, Tommy and his family in Hammersmith, Kate and Jean in Harlesden, the Edwards in Brixton, the Smiths and the Charles in Stoke Newington, the Douglases and the Hamiltons in Hackney, the Russells in Wembley, the Grants in Stonebridge, the Dorkings in Kensal Green, the Lowens and the Dodds in Paddington, the Ramsays and the Downings in Croydon, the Kings and the Campbells and the McKenzies in Southwark, the Gordons and the Johnsons in Birmingham, the Ashmeads in Luton, the St. Clairs in Reading, the Johnson's in High Wycombe, the Dunns in Wandsworth, the Duncans in Manchester, and in St. Albans the Nelsons, the Penants and the Bowmans.

As we met socially and in prayer, Ken and I advised that distance and time would not always allow us to meet and visit, but we encouraged them to start house groups and prayers: seek people out and begin evangelising to form local groups that would one day become local Church and community congregations.

This was to become the "Black Pentecostal Movement" as it was called*.

In time, combined groupings from various parts of Britain would meet in a hired school hall for what is called a Convocation. That is a church Service at which a lot of reassurance was given to each other through fiery evangelistic services where people were allowed to tell what they felt as born-again Christians, what they were doing, the prospects of their area and the mission

---

*See also *Partnership in Black and White* by Roswith Gerloff, Methodist Home Mission; *A Report on Afro-Caribbean Christianity in Britain* by Vanessa Howard, Leeds University Research Papers; and *Renewal*, March 1976, p 12, Fountain Trust.

ahead. It was difficult in those days even to get a school hall. Thank God, not many Pentecostals these days hold regular Church Services in a school. Very few use a Church hall. When the best can be obtained for the service of God, nothing less should be accepted. Most worship now in the Church itself.

These convocations were held from place to place, month by month, week by week, and every effort was made for a proper order to be kept so that each group would get their turn. So the group of people you saw in High Wycombe last week was sure to be in Stoke Newington next week, and at the same time some of the less committed black believers in those local areas would be there. Some of these patterns are still followed today, but to a lesser extent, as we are too many for all of us to go together these days and different kinds of leadership as well as growth have given local Churches strength to manage without the presence of other groups. Now there are less frequent united functions, such as Harvest Festivals, Anniversaries, Convocations, Funerals, Celebrations, Rallies, Conferences, Baptisms, Weddings, Ordinations, Inaugurations or the consecration of a new Church building.

ESTABLISHING

The Groups became Churches and leaders were found, who showed the capability, skill, call and desire to lead. Members of the group elected the leader and other Church officers. The leader must be happy to work with the officers and the officers must show obedience to the leader. That leader is the Minister. If there is more than one Minister, the Head Minister must approve the election of the others. If the person chosen as Head leader is not already an ordained Minister, he will be ordained by a Minister who has been ordained before. This ordainer would be brought from another branch, in the early days, to ordain the person becoming a Minister for the first time. Pentecostal Churches have leadership structures. Some have a Bishop, some do not. In some Pentecostal Churches the structure is: Apostles, Missionaries, Deacons, Evangelists, Pastors, Ministers. The Head Minister is the acting Bishop, until he is elected as Bishop or Archbishop. Another structure is: Missionaries, Deacons, Pastors, Overseers and Superintendent. Superintendent and Overseer in this structure are used at various levels: in local congregations, at district level, national level, as well as international levels.

No-one knew the way ahead. Only God knew. I worked hard, trusted God and followed as a man blinkered, handcuffed and being led. Some of us were to eat the sweet and some the bitter, but real prosperity was now to be seen. We began to see black people in minibuses with Bibles, ladies wearing lovely white gloves going to Church on Sundays in many towns. A transformation had really come. We felt that our hope, work and prayers, through one common faith in Christ, had been heard. The other amazing joy was that most of us now involved in faith and work had never met or even heard of each other before and would not have been likely to meet in any other way. This reminds me of the prophecy in *Zechariah**, in chapter 8 verses 7-8:

"This is what the Lord Almighty says, 'I will save my people from the countries of the east and the west. I will bring them back to live in Jerusalem; they will be my people and I will be faithful and righteous to them as their God.' "

*See *The Holy Bible* (NIV)

In 1962 my brother Ken and sister Monica decided to live nearer my sister Dorothy, Jean and my cousin Ruby, and various established new Church groups in London. Instead of using up time travelling, they would concentrate on worship and London evangelism and I would do more of the travelling. By the early 60s Ken was a Minister for a large group in Hornsey, still linking up with many groups round the North West, South West and South East regions, with many Pastors and Ministers emerging.

Pastoral and Ministerial meetings and United Services were being held. These were both necessary and useful. I was at all of them. I had opportunity to listen to the faith and views of other people and to help where I could. Everyone was accepted according to their own understanding. Not everyone, however, was able to accept all the views. Some strove for perfection and unity in doctrinal stance.

FACTIONS AND ELEMENTS

Some Pentecostals baptise in the name of the Father, the Son and the Holy Ghost, and some in the name of Jesus only. Most Pentecostals practise believer's baptism at an age when the individual concerned can understand. They do not Christen or baptise babies, but bless them.

One of the most brilliant, long-serving and well-trained Pentecostal Ministers, and one of the few who came to this country as an ordained Minister, felt there could be no departure from the full teaching of the Gospel of Jesus and the Apostles, and Jesus Christ the chief corner stone. He often quoted St. Paul's letter to the Galatians*: "Though we, or an angel from Heaven, preach any other Gospel unto you than that which we have preached unto you, let him be accursed." These words are in chapter 1, verse 8. These discussions presented us with a clear picture of varying interpretations by different groups and leaders. Many of these were very new and inexperienced leaders emerging, as well as some more experienced. The various interpretations had originated in the 1920s in Pentecostalism, with regard to Trinity and Oneness. These were to present new and varying factions.

It was becoming clear that there were three delicate matters to handle. Firstly each Pentecostal Minister was very frightened that someone who appeared to have far more eloquence than they considered themselves to have, might use a superior skill to take their leadership from them. Secondly we were going to have a distinctive Oneness faction. Thirdly, we were going to have a Trinitarian faction.

The same problems that started in the United States in the 1920s and followed in the Caribbean in the late 1920s, were again presenting themselves after the same pattern in Britain in the 1960s. I began to admonish everyone to relax the matter, carry on their respective work and not make these discussions so fluent and frequent, but continue to work as we had been doing, in unity.

*See *The Holy Bible* (AV)

I addressed these matters when setting up the International Ministerial Council of Great Britain** in 1968. I secured the autonomy of member Churches so that leadership and governance would not be threatened by outside agencies, and I made provision for Ministerial Training, both initial, formal studies and in-service training and discussion, so that by the guidance of the Holy Spirit working amongst us as we fellowshipped and spoke together we might be led into a deeper unity on all issues. By the same method in the ecumenical instruments I hope that differences among Christian traditions in the Churches in these islands will gradually become less divisive.

**See page 25

NEW THOUGHTS AND A WAY AHEAD

For the next few years the discussions of that kind were relaxed, not so much by deliberate intention but out of circumstances. A number of leaders, both of Oneness and Trinity, were beginning to make trips to USA and link or affiliate their small work in Britain to more established and older Pentecostal organisations in the States.
By 1966 a number of Bishops and Overseers from the States were coming to Britain to examine the prospects of work. They began to give financial support, even making small remuneration to Church leaders, as well as buying buildings for those who could accept being taken over. Until now the pattern has not changed. Some of the Pentecostal Churches here have headquarters in the United States and, more surprisingly, some of those headquarters are white-led. The majority of New Testament Trinitarians are American controlled. The Oneness, or more conservative independent Churches, tended to make a go of it on their own. Such assistance became a useful exercise and exchange. As a result we were blessed to have black pastors and theologians, such as Professor Gaymore, Professor Louis Charles Harvey and James Cone, and involvement from the Caribbean, Asia and Africa.

Notwithstanding all the growth and development within the Church, race relations had become a major problem since the highlighting of the problem in the Nottinghill Riots of 1958. An attempt to suppress the violence appeared to be an attempt to silence a volcano within the midst of those who thrive on racial hatred. This spread and intensified among people from all walks and all over the country, to become a hot brick to be held in the hands of people like myself, who seem to have been drawn in and left to pick up the pieces.

These elements have left caring leaders, both black and white, terrified and confused, and anxious to diffuse a time-bomb that was already set. Bodies like the West Indian Standing Conference, made up of people from the Caribbean who served here during the war, as well as some of us who were not involved in the second world war but were here as Commonwealth citizens to do a job and live in peace, were involved. Roy Jenkins was appointed as Home Secretary and Bonham Carter as Chairman of the Race Relations Board, to carry out the 1965 Race

Relations Act. The implementation of that Act was to leave an even worse taste in the mouths of the people the legislation was supposed to protect. Alas, the first person convicted under the 1965 Race Relations Act was a black man. That was Michael Malik Abdul X, a Black Power leader. He was convicted and sent to prison for incitement to racial hatred. That really worsened the climate and turned people against Race Relations legislation.

We were going to have to make our contribution to stick up for our rights, to seek independence through organisation and self-help. For a period I was going to concentrate on the formation of some sort of national Christian organisation to work at Church and community levels, and also another system of organisation to deal with race and education.

PREPARATIONS

It was now 1965. I decided to get to know personally more local white people who would accept me, work with and support me. I must understand their thinking and beliefs. I was made very welcome at Beechen Grove Baptist Church* by the Minister, Rev. Irwin Barnes, and by Deacon David Hillman and Deaconess Dorothy Fisk. Before long I became part of the Church and a worker within it. Within a few months I had brought five people to be baptised there, several children became members of the Sunday School, and many people became regular visitors and eventually entered into the fellowship. Beecham Grove had a very strong, hard working and loving Church team and they became a great asset in helping deprived and lonely people. Evangelism in our area was very successful, in particular among young people and young professionals.

There I was able to make a wide assessment. The race heat was so hot that even in such a loving and enthusiastic group of Christians, there were people

* In Watford

who were unhappy with the presence of black people.

This was not unknown to the Rev. Irwin Barnes and he did not pretend to brush it aside. He was so sensitive to the whole issue that when he and Mrs. Barnes were invited to an American Baptist Church as ambassadors from England and they found out that black Baptists and white Baptists did not worship together, they decided they could not continue with the exchange and returned home within a matter of days.

IN THE LOCAL TOWN 1967

My next move was to be involved in our local (Watford) Town Hall politics, as well as to get to know and become involved with our local M.P. who was the Rt. Hon. Raphael Tuck. Our first real involvement was early one Sunday morning, when we proceeded to Water lane and then to Radlett Road railway bridges to paint out graffiti written by racists about "wogs", "darkies" and "blackies". Several hundred people marched with us in support. That was the first sign of open victory. There were only four black people there. Everyone else was white. Among them were Communists, Christians, Liberals, Socialists, Conservatives, Agnostics.

The implication of the presence of black people in the community needed to be looked into. They needed a place to meet socially. There was discrimination in housing, education, employment and leisure facilities. The difficulty in getting local black children into grammar schools and complaints by black nurses in our local hospitals needed to be investigated.

First, we must invite a number of non-committed Church people to commit themselves to work with the committed Church: people who would not bring political ambition into our Church organisation but who would be aware of the very serious social, political and racial unrest this country was facing. They must realise, above all, the very dreadful threat hanging over black people who had settled here, while not failing to take account of how understanding white people wished the presence of black and new faces in Britain to work out happily and successfully to strengthen the workforce by replacing the manpower lost in the second world war. Also they should bear in mind that black people felt they had a duty to the "Mother country".

I felt I must, as a Christian leader, defuse the time bomb that was being wired up by a number of failures and serious blunders. We must, therefore, find committed people.

Next we must set up certain machinery to deal with the social and political aspects of the situation that faced the country and people. We must also have machinery that worked more within the boundaries of maintaining the Church at national levels, providing support among the growing Churches as they emerge, and finding ways of forming a link with the British Churches who saw the black Church groups as a new threat which might have to be removed.

Before all these, however, we must hold discussions with our local Town Hall as well as our Member of Parliament and bring to their attention the serious effect of the prevailing climate and the implications at the grass roots, with a view to canvas the wider support of members of the indigenous community and to help to educate those sections that needed to be educated, that the blacks in our presence were not a danger but wanted to be friends and helpers. Also they were here to stay.

Now it was our intention to go public. We were going to lobby every government Ministry and worthwhile organisation, industry and institution. We would make approaches to every area of society that we felt held power at any level. We were even going to discuss with the National Front who were a dangerous influence at the time, and also get the media to be involved in our cause.

TOWARDS NATIONAL CHURCH LINKS

It was now 1968. The Watford Bethel Apostolic Pentecostal Church had grown much larger than could be contained as a house to house Church group. Long discussions took place over two years with Miss G. Lawes, Headmistress of St. Andrews School, an old Church of England School building. She obtained permission from Herts County Council Education Department for us to hold services in the building. On 27th October 1968 the Bethel Apostolic Pentecostal Church Watford held its first local service in a public building. We had a full opening programme and a gathering of well over one hundred people. The reporter from the *Watford Observer* covered the service. The reporter wrote that it was the first time in her life she had seen so many coloured people at a local gathering, and the beautiful thing about it was that it was a Church service. The Church was now in the open and had a lot of support.

Now, as a Church in the local community, we must keep links nationally with the continuing programme of growth in the spreading of the Gospel and the freedom to allow Church leaders to emerge, as groups sprang up in various districts and towns. At the same time we had to work, where possible, with the British Churches to establish good relationships, to build up trust that would one day prove to be the building of bridges that was necessary.

We took action to form a Council to link the Churches at national level. Thus the International Ministerial Council of Great Britain was formed. Its objects are: to advance Christian education in the country of Great Britain, without discrimination on grounds of sex or race or

political, religious or other opinion; to provide facilities in the interest of Christian and social welfare, for recreation and leisure time occupation with the object of improving the conditions of a Christian life for the people. The Constitution, outlines of membership and administration and such matters were drawn up. The IMCGB was fully formed in 1968.* The IMCGB became an Associate member of the British Council of Churches(BCC) in July 1979.

LOCAL CONSULTATIONS

Our first meeting with officials of Watford Town Hall took place on 8th January 1969. We had to see how the local government officials, Town Hall people and local politicians would react to us and how we were going to find a way ahead. The meeting included Town Councillors and some Trade Union members. Before the date some officials, headed by Mr. Turner, Secretary to the Town Clerk's department, and two Town Councillors, Councillor Deakin and Councillor Gable, came to see me to tell me they had been going round the town doing a sort of referendum to find out who black people would pick to be a leader to meet all the unrest surrounding us in the community and in the country. They told me that everyone said it would have to be David Douglas. They asked me if I would attend the meeting on the 8th and I agreed. The meeting was chaired by Mr. Gordon Hall, the Town Clerk.

We discussed the problems of immigrants: housing, schools, jobs, trades unions, the Race Relations Act, the relationship of West Indians to the indigenous community, and the possible formation by me of an organisation to represent immigrant and other needs. This organisation, the Watford Race Representative Organisation (WRRO), was formed on 26 January 1969, having 12 representatives of immigrants from 12 countries. The terms of reference of each representative were to carry out the objectives of the first two clauses of the constitution. As Miss Paye later wrote, "Although founded by a West Indian, WRRO was never intended to be a pressure group for any one section of the people,

*See *UK Christian Handbook* 1987/88, pages 130 and 183

25

but to work to achieve justice for all. Membership from the first was always open to all and came to include people from every part of the West Indies, Pakistan, India, half a dozen European countries and the host community.

The aim of WRRO has always been to achieve justice, by identifying, and, wherever possible, remedying the causes of friction between varying sections of the population.

Now there was the Church, the International Ministerial Council of Great Britain and the Watford Race Representative Organisation. They were all part of the Church's function, but different departments. The function of WRRO, and later of UCWWA (United Church Welfare and Workers Association*), does not include the holding of Church Services, Prayer Meetings, Weddings, Funerals, Baptisms. They just do the wider community, social and humanitarian service that Christians and non-Christians need. We had now done all the organising of the various departments to do the work necessary to defuse what could be a racial time-bomb.

That work was easier said than done! We were now in the autumn of 1969 and had been struggling since 1958. The problems were growing every day. 1969 was just about the point at which the heights of racialism surfaced. Black people began to get cheesed off and were returning home. My brother Harry, my brother Leo and his wife Bernice, my sister Dorothy and her husband George, and my sister Monica and her husband had all gone. These were some of the people who had started in 1958.

*See p.80, and *UK Christian handbook 1987/88,* pages 130 and 183

SORROWS

Then came some disasters. There were two serious road accidents, one after the other. In the first, two brothers, close relatives of mine and part of our community, along with two children died. The survivors were the Mother, who was in a coma for a year, a boy who lost his eyes, a girl who was to become permanently paralysed and a boy who fully recovered. It was sad to perform funerals for the first time in a land so strange, where so many of us felt unwelcome. It certainly did add to the sorrows.

A few months later, a second accident followed almost the identical pattern. Again a cousin of mine and her husband were killed outright with one child. There were two other children severely injured, one paralysed for life. Another relative died also after the first bereavement as a result of shock. Everybody was looking to me for refuge, support, consolation and comfort.

A third tragedy in 1969 was the death of one of the key people in the life of all our Christian work. Mrs. Eslyn White, a candidate for baptism, died suddenly from meningitis. Racial tension was running so high that everything that happened aroused suspicions. The first thought was that the doctors did not do their job well because they were white and the patient black. A daily newspaper on Wednesday 16th April 1969 printed a report by David Wright carrying the headline: "Wife dies after her doctor says, 'Go home!'"

Mrs. Eslyn White died leaving five dependent children and a husband who had all moved from Jamaica only eighteen months previously. They had been apart for five years and had just moved into their new home. The townspeople were really angry. She had been well liked by everyone. She was a great loss to all. The black people felt the doctors could have done more. I had to talk with the coroners and doctors, and explain to the people that many factors that had caused the sad and sudden death of our dearly beloved Eslyn White. Whatever we might think, we were never going to bring her back. Besides Eslyn White would want things to be done calmly and with understanding.

I advised them to leave the matter to be investigated and if there should be a case to be answered, we would get that answer in due time. After the Coroner's report we advised the husband that there were no reasons to pursue a legal case. The people accepted what I told them.

To add to our sorrows, Mrs. Myrtle Llowellyn, a friend and workmate at Suede and Leathercraft Garment factory, died a few weeks later of the very same illness. The pattern of sorrows sometimes forms together to test and try the very people who would seem least able to bear and cope with such grief. It was not easy for the people. As for me, they saw my feelings and my determination to lead them to a type of rest to be found within. There came to me the sound of a song: "Are we weak and heavy laden, cumbered with a load of care? Jesus only is our refuge. Take it to the Lord in prayer." I called the people to prayer. I read to them the words of the Lord Jesus*, **"Come to me all you who are weary and burdened and I will give you rest. Take my yoke upon you and learn from me, for I am gentle and humble in heart, and you will find rest for your souls. For my yoke is easy and my burden is light."**

*The Holy Bible (NIV), Matthew 11: 28-30

CHAPTER TWO

Action

'The Lord replied, "Write the revelation and make it plain...... so that a herald may run with it."'

The Holy Bible (NIV), Habakkuk 2:2

IN THE NEWS
MOST EXTRAORDINARY
NOT CONVINCED

PREVENTATIVE MEASURES
HOUSING
INDUSTRY
EDUCATION

CIRCULATION AND EFFECTS
CORRESPONDENCE RESULTING FROM SURVEYS

IN THE NEWS

By 1969 the various departments of the Church and their activities were hitting the headlines of a number of newspapers, the *Watford Observer*, the *Evening Echo*, the *West Herts Post* and some of the national papers. Black Power extremists were trying to make trouble.

We knew that people cannot lead, either by causing trouble or by legitimate means, when they are a minority divided and do not have a proper, well-organised system with the power support of the people and resources. Strength and resources must come from the people of this country and we must get support from the host community if we were to climb over racial barriers.

Here are some of the headlines.

"Watford Attack on Racialists—Beware of Black Power, warns Watford Jamaican. Watford's growing coloured population was warned today against black power influences in Britain. The warning came from Jamaican-born David Douglas." That was the headline in a local paper in March 1969. The headline in another local paper said,
"I'll crush Town's black Power, Says Jamaican." Bob Freeman was reporting. "Jamaican Minister, David Douglas has formed an anti-Black Power movement in Watford." Both papers went on with a very lengthy story the next day.
Another reported, **"Watford's Growing West Indian Population is to get Bigger Say in Town's Affairs.** A 34-year old Jamaican Minister today announced the formation of a new body to represent his countrymen's views."

On 10th May the headline in two local papers read: **"Protest against Powell: Watford MP urged.** Watford MP Mr. Raphael Tuck has been urged to protest against Powellism, after Mr. Powell's speech last night in Wolverhampton on repatriation. A telegram came from Mr. Douglas, head of Watford Race Representative Organisation." Mr. Tuck certainly did protest and for the first time this matter was properly raised in Parliament.

Many things Mr. Powell predicted have come to pass, right here in the streets of some of our inner cities: race attacks and inner city riots in the streets of this country during the 1980s. Mr. Powell's speeches stirred up people who already had racial bias, half the time because they had no concept of what Mr. Powell's fears were. Having read Mr. Powell's autobiography, I understand why he thought as he did. He said painful things and he has paid the consequences of speaking too freely.

MOST EXTRAORDINARY

It was now 1970. There were lots of things to be done, but no-one was willing to listen and give honest assistance, unless it was political or commercial, or with prospect of fame for those who held power.

Then two extraordinary things happened.

Rev. Donald Eddie, a Methodist Minister, spoke out at a Church meeting in Oxhey. A local paper reported it, giving a small space to Mr. Eddie. A few Sundays later, Mr. Eddie invited me to his Church to preach and sing with my young people's group and a collection of £50 was made and given to me to help my work.

Then came the second happening.

Ann Paye, a historian and a Christian, came to work with me as General Secretary of WRRO. She was going to work voluntarily, full time, very long hours, at her own expense. It was by God's own mercies when I needed someone so well qualified, called and convicted.

She wrote to me in the Autumn of 1969 saying she had been reading about me and my work with great interest. We agreed to meet. I was cautious. I was under threat from extremists who used to telephone and write threatening letters. Sometimes the police had a safeguard watch on me if I knew I was going anywhere in public, like to a meeting. My cousin Rupert accompanied me to our meeting place in Hemel Hempstead. I was in for a surprise.

Miss Paye said, "I am glad your cousin has come with you, so that he too can hear." She had brought a number of books and papers to give me. There was a scrap book, notes, articles, history books and other educational books, Bibles and her bank book showing her life savings. All her life as a teacher she had saved that money. She was still a young woman. She said to me sadly, "I want you to have all these to help your work. They're no good to me. I'm dying of cancer. Even now I'm in terrible pain."

I questioned what, medically, had been done for her. She said, "It's no good. They can't do anything." We discussed her illness and her faith. I told her to keep her books and money and I prayed for her. When I had prayed she said, "Oh my God! My God! There is no pain! No pain for the first time in years! Praise the Lord!"

I warned her that the pain might return and that when it did she was to report to the hospital. Two days' later the pain did return and she reported to St. Joseph's, there to discover that Xrays showed that the cancerous growth had gone and she needed only a small operation to remove a tumour. Ann was home in a few days.

That was a miracle for Ann, who came to work with me in return for God's unfailing love and mercy, joining hands, heart and resources as black and white in partnership without any personal expectations. By 1970 Ann was deeply committed and she made a contribution over many years for which no prize can compensate.

NOT CONVINCED

We ran a supplementary school at St. Andrew's Hall in Watford; that is, a literacy and language school for people who were totally illiterate, those who could speak no English and those who were at school, but not doing well. We ran a day-to-day casework load to deal with people's problems. Our office was always in my home, a shed or garage in the garden or my front room.

At the heights of racial unrest, while the people who were in power, who were very well off and white, did not think there was a problem, there were two types of black people who did not see a problem. There were those who were on their way home, and those who did cheap labour jobs involving long night shifts that no-one else would want to do. These would sleep all day long, go nowhere, have no pleasure and take part in nothing, because they intended to leave the country in four or five years' time. For most of us, however, this country was going to be home for life.

They told Mr. Enoch Powell the same thing – about going home. Indeed Mr. Powell, a very serious man, took it seriously and felt, if this is the case, these people really do not mean to stay, they have come just to grab what they can and go back home. He suggested the government should give them a sum of money and let them go. That is what they came for. That is why he suggested voluntary repatriation.

A meeting was held by a left-wing Black Power group. They invited Councillors from the three major parties: Conservatives, Labour and Liberal. The Councillors were trying to say there were no racial problems in Watford. It was reported in February 1970 in a local paper with the headline: **No Race Strain in Watford.** At that meeting I pointed out that there were no major complaints because, although we had a 1960 and 1962 Commonwealth Immigrants Act and Race Relations Acts of 1965 and 1968, they were ineffective. I was very sure that if there was no race problem, then the meeting was purposeless, unless there was a hidden agenda.

The newspapers reported: **Dramatic Rival Factions.**

PREVENTATIVE MEASURES

The time had come to produce more serious evidence of areas of discrimination, in order to prevent the worst from coming, rather than wait for the worst to come and then try to deal with it. We decided to do surveys in three main areas of need, in the immediate immigrant community and among the people as a whole, to try to see how the black immigrants, as well as other sections of the community, were affected.

We proceeded with immediate action to carry out surveys into the following: 1. Local production and manufacturing industry; 2. Housing: rent, lease, purchasing and sales; 3. Schools: infant, primary, secondary. Miss Ann Paye, historian and former school teacher and an English person, Miss Josephine James, a former school teacher from Kingston, Jamaica, and myself, did the survey of industries. Larry Gibson, a young school teacher from Watford, and his wife Gill, took housing. Ann Paye and Josephine James did the schools' survey. The schools' survey commenced after the schools returned from the summer holidays and was completed on 21st September 1970. The industrial survey commenced in autumn 1970 and was completed on 14th April 1971. The housing survey commenced in spring 1971 and ended on 18th November 1971.

HOUSING

There was clear discrimination in most aspects of renting a house. First, letters were written to Estate Agents representing a white person's interest and also, at the same time, a black person's interest. In 99% of cases the white person would be successful. In run-down digs the black person's chance of success rose to about 20%. In house buying there were no boundaries to a white person or restrictions by vendors, but blacks were put off by agents if, say, they wanted to buy a house in Cassiobury Estate, unless it was discovered they were someone like Sidney Poitier or Sammy Davies Junior. Even then the vendors might feel the neighbours might not be happy about it. Agents were quick to recommend sales to blacks in over-crowded areas. With both lease and sale, discrimination was at the same level, except for shops in ghetto-type areas where shops were easily obtained by blacks.

INDUSTRY

As for jobs in factories and offices, dirty jobs were easy to obtain if the black person would have them in spite of the fact that he was skilled. Some very highly-skilled black workers had to take very poor semi-skilled jobs and work twice as hard for a lower rate of pay, with the hope that a good Director or General Manager might come to realise what that black worker was really capable of doing. Once that barrier was broken, then opportunity would come. This was one of my personal experiences too, so when the survey revealed this I was not surprised. Promotion and apprenticeships for blacks were few and far between. There were no black foremen, charge-hands, managers, supervisors or Union Shop Stewards. It was no better among the local Town hall staff. Looking deeper into the analysis, however, we felt that high technical skills resulting from good training and better understanding would one day vanquish discrimination in industry. Notwithstanding, for various reasons, discrimination in industry was about 60% taking into account the many and varied factors.

EDUCATION

The survey shows no discrimination in Infant Schools, either by teachers or by pupils; but there was discrimination by parents picking up children, complaining to the teacher and saying who they did and did not want their child to play with. The Headmistress generally ignored the request. At Primary School there was a slight variation. There was no discrimination by teachers, but some children were prompted at home, possibly by racist parents, to call black children names in school. Those children who suffered verbal aggression might fight back and this always caused teachers a lot of concern. However, the children overcame the difficulties among themselves.

In Secondary Schools a small number of individual teachers were found to be racially biased as well as prejudiced. They discriminated largely on political conviction, religious convictions or agnosticism. Half the time they were not aware of the effects of their attitudes. This had been the case with Enoch Powell who clearly did not realise the effects of his beliefs on other people. Another handicap for the black child was that, having grown up without the things and a whole way of life that were normal for a white child, the black child had to learn those things in class while, at the same time, trying to compete with and keep up with the white children. This had unfortunate results. Black children became over-pressurised, overworked and fell further and further back, at the same time slowing down the white children who had far less to do in more time during the school day. The teachers then became confused and sometimes neglected the black children, just leaving them to fall behind in their lessons. Then they claimed that they were slow or educationally subnormal (ESN). **Black parents were up in arms and the school, the children and the teachers were blamed. Then most people ran away with the ideas either that it was all caused by racialism or that black children are not intelligent, or that teachers do not care. Every good teacher, however, wants to turn out the best pupils, whatever their race or colour.**

CIRCULATION AND EFFECTS

The time had come to circulate the surveys to local and statutory Government departments as well as to the press and local authority; to set up a Community Relations' Council (CRC); to do something to improve the poor housing conditions in the town; to combat racism; to monitor employment measures with the aim to make them better and fairer; and to assist the system of education by creating machinery in schools to deal with the new problems they faced.

Survey results were sent to the following industries and bodies: The Department of Education and Science, Hertford Education Authority, the Greater London Council, Sir Keith Joseph as Minister for Education, The Minister for Trade and Industry, the Ministry for Employment and Productivity, the Department of Health and Social Services (DHSS), The Prime Minister Mr. Heath, The Home Secretary Mr. Reginald Maudling, Leader of the Opposition Mr. Harold Wilson, the Trades Union branches at local level, the Community Relations Commission who replaced the Race Relations Board, the Liberal Party, the CBI, the Commonwealth High Commissions, the British Council of Churches, individual MPs and Junior Ministers.

The Housing Report by Larry and Gill Gibson was first to hit the headlines of the local papers on 15th October 1971. The headline was: **"Needed Now: Town Warned About Future."** Bodies that had been circulated replied with praise, gratitude and support. All this greatly assisted our case and the local Borough conceded that a CRC was necessary. My next move was to invite the Regional Development Officer for the South, Errol Dickerson, the local MP, the Rt. Hon. Raphael Tuck, the High Commissioners of Jamaica, Trinidad and Guyana, members of the three local political parties, the Town Councillors, Heads of the various Church organisations and members and Heads of local voluntary organisations to a meeting with a Caribbean feast. All the beautiful, leading black women of the town came to cook and wait on our guests.

The meeting was held at the Co-op Hall in Watford. It was filled to the bottom of the stairs. Our MP Mr. Raphael Tuck, Mr. Errol Dickerson, the Community Relations Commission Regional Development Officer, Mr. Alan Ray, Guyana High Commissioner and Mr. Alan Burgar, the Jamaican High Commissioner, were the main speakers. Then it was time for questions and contributions. The meeting saw clearly that, in response to the reports, everyone conceded that there was overwhelming support for the setting up of a CRC in Watford.

Within a few months we were having monthly meetings in the town with a temporary body called the Immigrants Advisory Group. From this point the Town Hall took the responsibility to set up the Watford CRC, with our help and support. I was the Co-Chairman of the Watford CRC for five years. A Community Relations Officer was employed and that was one problem left behind. I thank God that those determined efforts were made. **Life was improved in Watford. We have not, so far, had a serious race problem and I do not foresee one because we woke up early. This was accomplished through work and leadership and fairness in action and judgement, as well as by faith in God and coming in contact with the right people at the right time.**

CORRESPONDENCE RESULTING FROM SURVEYS

I will now bring you up to date with some of the many things that happened between 1969 and 1971.

We had to pay attention to many important issues. These were: better race relations, freedom and liberty in housing, education and employment irrespective of race, colour, sex or religion, and the need for equal opportunity to be considered in all aspects. We laid great emphasis on old age pensioners and those who were deprived through lack of opportunity, for with opportunity many people would make some headway to help themselves as well as others.

Here is a letter dated 2nd June 1971, from the Department of Health and Social Security. "I have been asked to reply to your letter of 21st April addressed to the Secretary of State for Social Services.

"The Government propose to increase the single rate of retirement pension by £1-00 per week and the rate for a married couple by £1-60 per week in September. The increase will be the largest ever.

"The Government also intend to increase the old persons' pensions provided under the National Insurance Act 1970 from £3-00 a week for a single person and £1-85 for a married woman, to £3-60 and £2-20 respectively as from the week commencing 20th September..........(The letter continued to list pension increases for other categories of people)........

"It can be said with confidence that the new rates of pension will have a higher real value than the present rates had when they were introduced in 1969.

"As you will appreciate, the important question of the well being of the elderly is not simply one of pension rates. Health and welfare facilities are also most important and the Government have already announced a substantial increase in the loan sanction facilities available to bring about improvements in these services.

"You can rest assured, therefore, that the Government have all aspects of the needs of the elderly much in mind."

We received the following reply from Mr. Errol Dickerson of the Community Relations Commission when we sent our survey on industry to that office. "Thank you for your letter of 5th June, and for the very comprehensive survey of industries in your area.

"The information is crucial to our work and should certainly serve as a guide for future developments in Watford.

"I wish to personally compliment you and Mr. Douglas for the thoughtful questionnaire you arranged and I should at the same time be similarly complimentary to the firms who gave you their co-operation.

"As you may know, I have already submitted my report on Watford to the Commission and should be in touch with you as soon as I know the findings."

We also studied the freedom of people joining the Common Market, as to how the Treaty of Rome would affect people of the Commonwealth countries. Clause 3 of Articles 48-49 of the Treaty placed certain difficulties in the way of some people, particularly those of black Commonwealth countries.

We wrote to Mr. Heath and received this reply dated 15th May 1972. "Your letter of 14th May to Mr. Heath has been copied to this department (Immigration and Nationality) for reply on the points raised with regard to the Treaty of Rome.

"Articles 48 and 49 of the Treaty provide for the freedom of movement for workers within the European economic Community. This entails the abolition of any discrimination on the grounds of nationality between workers of the Member States, as regards employment, remuneration and other conditions of work and employment. This means that workers of the Member States of the Community may compete for jobs on equal terms with British subjects and resident labour, either black or white, and you may be assured there is no question of racial discrimination in this matter."

The first reply, dated 4th May 1972, to our letter about the Treaty of Rome, also contained information about an Urban programme. "A new phase of the Urban Programme is due to be announced in the very near future, and it is open to you to apply for grant aid, although I cannot of course say whether or not any application you make will be successful. I enclose a note explaining the conditions etc. for Urban Programme aid which you may find useful."

We studied the police and how they investigate. We wanted to know what right police had to call at an immigrant's house, kick down his door and arrest his family, to find out later that they were all innocent. There were various issues. Some people break the law because of malicious racial bias, while others break the law because the law was made against their status. Immigrants were investigated although they had broken no law and were put to serious disadvantage and agony. When we wrote to the Home Secretary on this subject, we received this reply, dated 26th April 1972.

"I am sorry to have taken so long to reply to your letter to the Home Secretary of 2nd March about investigating organisations.

"First, let me say that the Home Secretary is glad to know of the activities of all organisations working towards harmonious community relations. Immigrants themselves have a major part to play in achieving this objective. There are inevitably individuals, both in the host population and in the immigrant communities, who do not share this goal. However, so long as they keep their activities within the law they are free to express their views, and it would be quite wrong for the police or the Home Office to interfere.

"The Home Secretary is satisfied that Chief Officers of Police have the necessary power to investigate organisations and individuals who are suspected of breaking the law. In any event the responsibility for deciding what course of action should be taken as a result of an investigation rests with the Chief Officer of Police and the Home Secretary has no power to intervene and direct what course of action should be taken."

The surveys we did found wide acceptance and led to further discussion, as these replies show.

The first is dated 16th June 1971 and is from the Department of Employment at 168 Regent Street. "Thank you for your letter of 7th June sending us a report of the industrial survey carried out by your organisation.

"Mr. Haworth, who is head of the section in this Department which deals with its policy in race relations in employment and with its functions under the Race Relations Act 1968, is on holiday at present. I am sure that he will be most interested in your report and will contact you on his return about a mutually suitable date for a discussion."

The second is dated 16th August 1971 and is from the Eastern and Southern Regional Office of the Department of Employment. "I recently had the opportunity to see the report of a survey carried out by your organisation among employers in Watford, which you sent to the Secretary of State for Employment.

"Your report reached me because my work includes responsibility for employment advisory matters in the Watford area, and I should be glad to discuss its contents with you. If you agree, perhaps you could contact me and we can arrange to meet."

I received replies and thanks from other Government Departments and Ministers, but this sample is sufficient for my purpose.

CHAPTER THREE

In the Public Eye

"Faith by itself, if it is not accompanied by action, is dead."

The Holy Bible (NIV), James 2:17

QUICK ACTION IN 1971
ACTION UNDERWAY
THE DAY APPROACHES

DO SOMETHING ABOUT MR. POWELL!
CHALLENGING THE NATIONAL FRONT
WATFORD COMMUNITY RELATIONS COUNCIL

THE PRESS AND ITS DRAMATISATION
RELATIVES INTERVENE

QUICK ACTION IN 1971

The 1971 Immigration Act would have caused a near revolution. We had in Britain a 1948 Immigration Act, a 1972 Commonwealth Immigrants Act and Race Relations Acts of 1965 and 1968. In spite of all the weaknesses of past laws, none had provoked a reaction like that which Clause 4 of the 1971 Immigration Bill would have produced. Clause 4 would have made the immigrant population carry identity cards and in many ways would have revoked their rights. They could have been asked at any time to produce the document, and some would have had to be registered with the police as well as report to their local police at specified times. The police would have been forced to take action that could only worsen what was already a very bitter fruit. The Police Department, under Sir Robert Marks, had already made it clear that they were unhappy about Clause 4, should it become law. The immigrant population was clearly outraged. Quick and positive measures had to be taken to prevent this bill, which would turn fear into discrimination by legislation, from receiving its final reading and becoming law.

Every organisation that realised the very wide implications behind the proposed law had voiced their concern. A meeting was called by the West Indian Standing Conference, with Mary Dines, Secretary of the National Joint Council for the Welfare of Immigrants, Joe Hunt of the West Indian Standing Conference, and Len Dyke, who sent out the invitations, for us to plan ways and means to deal with the very serious concerns the Bill had brought to the most vulnerable members of the community. At the Standing Conference were Trade Union members, ex-service men, community workers, the National Union of Students, political party members and others. They elected me and gave me the task of organising a National Day of Mourning in protest against Clause 4. It was to take place on 24th October 1971, which was United Nations Day. That year was United Nations Year against Racial Discrimination.

I was given the help of Gil Gibson, Secretary of the National Union of Students and Ann Paye, the General Secretary of WRRO, but no money, no equipment and no planning advice as to how to get this uphill, if not impossible, task off the ground.

Joe Hunt, Mary Dines, Len Dyke and Satunie Williams and others were to take charge of the political side of the Day of Mourning with lobbying.

The West Indian Standing Conference(WISC) is an umbrella organisation based at 30 Georges House, Gunthorpe Street, London E1, made up of many West Indian organisations, each with three delegates to represent their views and interests at the Conference. At that time Joe Hunt B.A. was Secretary and Len Dyke was Chairman. Two large meetings were held with the WISC to plan the National Day of Mourning. These were held on 22nd June and 3rd July 1971. After the July meeting the work started for Ann Paye, Gil Gibson (no relation of Larry Gibson) and me. We three met at a Watford evening dinner and planned our action, to be ready by the last week of July to start our campaign and gain support for October 24th. My letter was ready by 18th August 1971. Here is the wording of the letter:
"Dear Friends, I write to ask your help in a special national protest against the Immigration Bill, a piece of legislation which will affect all of us, of whatever faith. You may already have taken part in public meetings against the Bill during its passage through Parliament, but I hope that the idea of a National Day of Mourning will get the support of your members.

"The Immigration Bill cannot now be passed until Parliament reassembles in November; meanwhile there are Party conferences next month at which it may be totally obscured by the issue of the Common Market. We do not want this Bill to slip into the statute book in this way; and we believe there is a need to show through the press and the mass media that the majority of people resent its racist effects.

"At a recent meeting sponsored by the Joint Council for the Welfare of Immigrants and a number of youth, immigrant and religious organisations, we came up with the idea of a Day of Mourning as one which is of a solemn religious nature. October 24th is U. N. Day and this year is supposed to be the U.N. Year Against Racial Discrimination; we believe it would be cynical to celebrate October 24th as a day of world community if the Immigration Bill, which is a racialist Bill, is introduced a month later.

"Would you, therefore, be able to play some part in the Day of Mourning on October 24th? You will, of course, know best what kind of activity is most appropriate for you. Even an individual could contribute by wearing a black armband or by distributing leaflets outside his place of worship. But we are hoping that religious organisations will play a very important role. Perhaps, for example, you could lay a wreath at a central point in the town; preach a 'sermon', conduct a symbolic 'mock' funeral in your religious tradition. Whatever is possible we would be grateful if you would keep us informed, so that we can give a national picture to the press and radio in advance, telling them of your activity and explaining that we are mourning the death of a public commitment by government to the value of a multi-racial Britain.

"I am writing to Churches of all faiths, both nationally and in your town, to ask for their co-operation; only if many people help will the idea get over to the general public and to the Government. Please work together on this solemn protest.
"I look forward to hearing your views and activities."

ACTION UNDERWAY

By the end of August 441 religious organisations had been sent a copy of my letter. Postage stamps were only three pence (three old pennies!) at the time. The printers were quite happy to give envelopes at cost price and we had an old-time duplicator to copy the letters. Letters were sent to the Home Secretary, Mr. Maudling, the Prime Minister, Mr. Heath, the Foreign and Commonwealth Department and Members of Parliament. Apart from the 441 religious organisations, we circulated

50 civic organisations and 8 Church Newspapers. Other newspapers were free to pick up the news by themselves.

We also wrote a letter on 23rd March to the Prime Minister about the Immigration Bill and received the following reply dated 6th April 1971:

"Dear Mr. Douglas and Miss Paye, As you know a copy of your letter of 23rd March to the Prime Minister has been passed to this office.

"Your letter raised certain points on clause 4(3) of the Immigration Bill, which concerns the power to require a person who has been given leave to enter the United Kingdom for a limited period to register with the police.

"The Bill and the draft Immigration Rules provide that Commonwealth citizens who come here for employment are to be required to register with the police until they are accepted for permanent settlement, which would normally be after four years in approved employment. People coming here from outside the Commonwealth for employment, or as students or long term visitors, will also be required to register, as they are at present.

"Registration involves giving the police, on arrival, certain information, e.g. name, age, nationality, address – and subsequently notifying them of any change of address or employment. In the Metropolitan Police District, in which about half the present registrations of aliens are effected, the initial registration is carried out at the Aliens Registration Office in Holborn, which is manned entirely by civilian staff. In large provincial cities, too, there are special aliens registration offices, manned wholly or partly by civilian staff.

"The system has worked satisfactorily for many years in relation to people coming from countries outside the Commonwealth, and the Government does not think its extension to certain Commonwealth citizens, as proposed under the Bill, should give rise to the sort of problems mentioned by the Organisation. But, as the Home Secretary said during the debate on the Second Reading of the Bill, he

**is ready to consider any alternative arrangements for registration which would be practicable and effective, and the suggestion made by your Organisation will be born in mind.
Yours sincerely, D. Roberts."**

We include the complete wording of these letters, to show that the Government Departments genuinely believed that the Government had got it right in legislation in previous laws that affected coloured people, and they truly expected it all to go unnoticed by the people of this country who understood what it meant if the legislation remained law and if the 1971 Bill, Clause 4, should become law. They thought it would go unnoticed by both white and black people who really cared.

By the first week of September 1971 the replies of those who were in support of the Day of Mourning, as well as a few who were not, began to reach my office in Watford. By 2nd September the Jewish Chronicle, the Church Times, Lambeth Palace, the Salvation Army, the Presbyterian Church of England, the Seventh Day Adventist Church, the Baptist Union of Great Britain and Ireland, the Society of Friends, the Bishop of Birmingham, the Bishop of St. Albans, the Bishop of Nottingham, the Bishop of Stepney, Trevor Huddleston, the Hertfordshire Constabulary, the Communist Party of Great Britain, the British Council of Churches, the local Roman Catholic Church, Holyrood, St. Dominicans, St. Joseph's, the Holy Ghost Fathers and the Orders of the Sisters of the Poor, the Congregationalists, the Pentecostals, the Methodist Church, Oxford Students, local and County Councillors, some Dublin Churches, the Italian Baptists, and many religious groups, Muslim and Sikh, voluntary organisations and people from all over the country were writing to us in support. They did many helpful things to make me and my colleagues feel encouraged. Then I knew, out of what had seemed a hopeless situation, for so many people had told me that even if anything could have been done we had left it too late, now there was hope, and we had been at work long before our critics had realised.

THE DAY APPROACHES

We were now ready to see the big day come on October 24th. The Department of the Environment had written to us as follows:

"The Cenotaph is a Memorial specifically dedicated to the fallen in the 1914-18 and 1939-45 wars. I am afraid that the occasion you have in mind would not be suitable there and I regret, therefore, that the required permission cannot be given on this occasion."

We decided to lay the wreath within sight of the Cenotaph on October 24th. Then on 23rd October I received a letter from the Home Office, signed by Mrs. E. I. France and dated 20th October, in reply to my letter containing our plan for the National Day of Mourning. It read:

"Dear Mr. Douglas, I have been asked to reply to your letter of 7th October to the Home Secretary concerning the Immigration Bill. As you may have heard, the Government announced in the House of Lords on 11th October that no Commonwealth citizen will be required to register with the police and have said that the Immigration Rules will be amended accordingly."

The announcement was received with joy and celebration and prayers of thanksgiving. We began to telephone and write to tell Churches and Organisations not to proceed with actions as planned. Some people had seen the news, but some were not sure exactly what it actually meant. We were able to reach about 90% in time, but the remaining 10% carried out the actions they had planned. We received letters later telling us what they had done and what the outcome had been.

DO SOMETHING ABOUT MR. POWELL!

We continued to watch and work locally and nationally as a self-help body, working as close as we were allowed with all the relevant Government and voluntary organisations. We never hid our reservations but always shared the difficulties with concern to do what we could. We shall continue to work in that way as long as the voice of the Church remains one of the ways in which man can share and live in peace together, by love, caring, patience and understanding.

There had been some controversial experiences centring round the 1970 General Election and continuing into 1971 with the unrest caused by the 1971 Immigration Bill, Clause 4. Mr. Powell, MP for Wolverhampton, discovered how sensitive people were when the immigrant population became outraged by his pre-election speeches*, or at least by what people at the time interpreted those speeches to mean. How was the host community, who voted in the election, responding? We waited for a reaction from all levels of society. A general meeting was called of the working departments of the Churches, the leaders of those bodies and the membership. Decisions were made that I had to do something about Mr. Powell, as well as the National Front.

The election delayed things, and in any case Mr. Powell's party won the election.

Many black people voted for Mr. Powell in Wolverhampton in 1970. Notwithstanding, WRRO sent a report to the Home Secretary about the rise in temperature resulting from Mr. Powell's speeches and voicing concern that racial disorder could be provoked. The Home Secretary, Mr. Maudling, assured us in his reply that our report was looked at by both the Foreign Office and the Home Office.

The Foreign Office received our report on 28th January 1971. Copies had been passed to them by the Home Office who acknowledged that they received it on 21st October 1970. Not much came from Mr. Maudling, except that he tried to assure us that everything will be done for the immigrants here and that all must and will be treated fairly, as far as the government could find it possible. The police would deal with any disturbance to protect everyone in these islands.

We drew attention during this period to the fact that, in spite of Race Relations legislation, Mr. Powell could speak as he did, and he and others could aggrieve immigrant people and get away with it.

*Extracts from 5 election speeches of Mr. Powell are contained in *Mr Powell and the 1970 Election,* published by Elliot Right Way Books, SBN 7160 0551 4.

This is the reply from the Home Office to these criticisms of ours in a letter of 4th December 1971.

"It is the Government's declared policy that all citizens should be treated as equal before the law and without discrimination. We fully realise the important contribution that immigrants have made in this country and are anxious that they should develop their skills to the full, acquire social and economic status to which their skills entitle them and play a full part in social and political life. It is realised, however that there are some immigrants, although not the majority, who wish to keep their own culture and way of life as far as this is possible. It is not our wish to try to force them to conform in every respect to the British way of life.

"I am afraid that we cannot agree with your statement that legislation against racial discrimination is unhelpful. **The purpose of the 1968 Race Relations Act was to ensure that people were not treated unfairly because of their race or colour in fields such as employment, housing and the provision of goods and services.** The Race Relations Board has had some success in enforcing the law in this matter, while the Community Relations Commission, which was set up under the 1968 Act to promote harmonious community relations on a national basis, also has a record of worth while achievement. If you would care to read the annual reports of the Board and the Commission, which are published by the Stationery Office, you would, I think, be able to assess more accurately the contribution which they are making to the well being of our society.

"You urge Government action to remedy the disadvantages suffered by coloured immigrants but you do not seem aware of the positive action which is already being taken. Under the Local Government Act 1966 the government makes grants available to those local authorities which have to employ staff specially to deal with social problems arising from differences of language and culture. There is also an Urban Programme for making additional financial assistance available to areas of special social need. Many of these are also places where there is a high concentration of immigrants, and they benefit from the programme. In the field of education, extra teachers and additional equipment are being promoted for the teaching of English to immigrant school pupils while many local education authorities also make special arrangements for teaching English to older immigrants. As regards employment, the Department of Employment and Productivity is pursuing, with a considerable degree of success, its policy of promoting non-discrimination. Since the passing of the Race Relations Act few employers have imposed discriminatory restrictions on vacancies, but, when this does happen, all possible efforts are made to persuade the employer to change his practice. If these fail the services of the employment exchange may be withdrawn from the firm.

"The above are some of the main positive measures being taken by the government. The only additional specific suggestion which you make is that steps should be taken to ensure that coloured people hold jobs in every organisation in Great Britain. This gives the impression that people should be selected for jobs according to the colour of their skin. This of course is quite contrary to our policy which is that applications for jobs should be considered solely on the basis of an applicant's education, ability and qualifications regardless of his race or colour."

People in government genuinely believed that their policy was right.

The election was won and Mr. Powell settled once again in Parliament. Once more he made some of his dramatic speeches. I wrote to Mr. Powell at the House of Commons, but he did not reply. The letter from me to Mr. Powell was very cool and friendly. A copy of it was sent to the Prime Minister, Mr. Heath. Mr. Douglas Hurd, Political Secretary, sent this reply, dated 17th March 1971.

"Mr.Powell speaks for himself, not for the Conservative Party, and not for the Government. The Prime Minister has made this clear on a very large number of occasions, and he hopes that it is fully understood by all the members of your organisation.

"**Mr. Heath has also made clear his determination that everyone settled here should enjoy equality before the law, and that there should be no first and second class citizens in Britain.** The Government have kept this principle firmly in mind in preparing the Immigration Bill which is now before the House of Commons."

CHALLENGING THE NATIONAL FRONT

In August 1971 the National Front campaigned to convert more people to their cause. The National Front launched a campaign against a Mr. and Mrs. Peters* of Potters Bar who were fostering black children. The National Front claimed that neighbouring houses would fall in value if black people were allowed to live in the area, and they tried to get the residents to sign a petition against the Peters. The Front called a

*The editor has changed the name for reasons of privacy protection.

meeting and well over a hundred people met at a hall in Potters Bar. Members of the Race Relations Board were present and various newspaper reporters and the Peters family in their defence. I walked into the hall with Ann Paye. We had a tape recorder and our notebooks. I set up my tape recorder and waited at the back. I had on my clerical collar. After we had waited for a while John Tyndall, Martin Webster and Peter Applin, the three officials, walked in to commence the meeting.

Members of the Race Relations Board were there to observe. They could not take any action or give any evidence that would be of any value in law. No-one would realise that the Race Relations Board were there, nor would they be aware of Ann Paye, because these people were white. However, there were eyes staring at me from all corners. Two men went up and whispered to John, Peter and Martin. They came over to me immediately and asked if I was the Rev. David Douglas. One of them said. "Rev. you must surely have lots of guts to come here! We don't think you're going to like what will take place here. We wouldn't advise you to stay."

Another said, "You can't tape the meeting. Can you turn it off?"

I said, "No."

He said, "We are very sorry, we are going to have to switch your machine off." He stretched out a hand to do so.

John Tyndall then called loudly to the man, "No! Leave him! Leave his recorder alone!"

Then John commenced the meeting like this, "We have to welcome a very different person among us tonight. Rev. David Douglas is to be praised for his bravery and I want him to be treated well in our midst. Our policies are that we don't hate black people. We are saying that this country is for white people and Africa and the Caribbean and India are for the blacks. If I go to India or Africa I would hope to be treated well for the short period as a guest, but the problems here in Britain are different. The blacks have come to take over and change our country and our very life style. Rev. Douglas knows that." With words such as those he opened the meeting. Then he said, " May I ask him (meaning me), since he knows the truth, why has he come to this meeting?"

I replied that I had an interest, and as long as no laws were broken, my presence at this meeting would be the same as at any other. But if the law was infringed, WRRO would seek to report the matter to the Race Relations Board by the transcript of what was said.

Mr. Tyndall understood where we both stood. He gave his speech and, in my view, he did not break any of the laws, neither the 1965 Act nor the 1968 Act. Martin Webster then gave a speech in this vein: that the blacks came to this country because they were lazy. They had gold in their land, rubies, diamonds and wealth, but they were just lazy and too stupid to get it even when it was at their feet. Now that we have gone and taken it from their feet and made good and proper use of it, they have come to take it away. We can't sit by and allow that. They crowd our streets. The houses are devalued. Muck and dirt is all over where they are, so this country will soon be like where they came from, run-down, poor, riddled with crime. It will be worse here when they eat our food and drink our milk and all our rich things. They breed like rabbits and we will all be finished. We must prevent this. That is why we are here tonight.

A report was made against the National Front. A case was brought against them by the Race Relations Board. The transcript taken by us at that meeting was used as the correct evidence of the meeting. In August 1971 Peter Applin and Kenneth Taylor were found guilty under Section 12 of the 1968 Race Relations Act. The Front members merely paid a fine.

It did not end just there with the National Front. We tried very seriously to talk with their leader, John Tyndall, to reason out the folly of the Front with logic and understanding. BBC radio invited myself and John Tyndall to a face to face discussion on the radio for the people of Britain. We both agreed. I got there. The Directors set all things ready, but John failed to arrive. Then the WRRO invited the National Front to meet them at St. Andrews Hall, Watford. Again they did not come. They told the newspapers that they understood that there were lots of protests launched against them. The final meeting, arranged by Ann

Paye, was just for me and John Tyndall to meet in Watford. He again agreed. Again he did not come. I received a letter a few days later from John Tyndall telling me how he had been attacked on the way and his car turned over.

Mr. Martin Webster, the front-line Co-ordinator of the Front's activities, had appealed against the prosecution that followed the 1971 meeting, wishing to take it further and reverse the action and ruling of Judge Rustle. Lord Denning, Master of the Roll, refused permission for an appeal to the House of Lords. Lord Denning made a point that Ken Taylor and Peter Applin had invited Mr. Peters to discriminate against the children, although the incitement charges had not succeeded in the previous hearing of the case. According to Section 12 of the 1968 Act, "a person who deliberately aids, induces or incites another to do an act which is unlawful…….shall be treated as doing the act."

WATFORD COMMUNITY RELATIONS COUNCIL

The surveys carried out by WRRO in education, industry and housing were intended in the first place to inform government departments and agencies so that they might be able to understand and form a nationwide picture of human need. Their other purpose was to encourage the local Council of Watford that the town needed a Community Relations Council. Some Councillors and Town Hall officials were saying there was no need and how good things were. We had to show them that to those who live in heaven all things are bright and beautiful; but to those who are down and out, it is hell on top, hell underneath, and in between it is hot and impossible. The people who were in office and in power were privileged not to see the need for a CRC in Watford. Two years it took them to read and study our various reports and look at the volume of work that had been done, although they had been holding frequent meetings under the name of the Immigrants Advisory Sub-committee. This was made up of Watford Borough Council, Watford Race Representative Organisation, the Indian Workers Association, Watford Trades Council, the Young Volunteer Force Foundation, the Divisional Education office, Watford Police, the Employment Exchange, the Social Service Department, District Manufacturing Association and the Citizens Advice Bureau.

We had been using this group to act as judges who would deal with the questions raised by our campaign for better race and community relations in the town, as well as other parts of the country. By Friday 2nd June 1972 the Advisory Committee was looking at the needs report the Working Party had prepared on 17th May 1972 and estimates of the cost of the formation of a CRC. I was also on that Advisory Committee and on the Working Party and that helped to expedite matters and make things much easier.

The Community Relations Commission, when looking at my survey report, promised that they would take the matter up with Watford Borough Council. This they did, and Miss Nadine Pepard and Mr. Mark Bonham Carter (it was later David Lane) had been to see the Borough Council in connection with the reports and the setting up of a CRC in Watford. By 24th January 1973 a membership drawn from various organisations in the town was invited to serve on Watford Community Relations Council. The Watford CRC was formed by early February and by March 1973 we were seeking to employ the first Community Relations Officer.

After all the preparation the CRC did not do the work that needed to be done, the work it was set up to do. The Nadine Pepard – Bonham Carter – David Lane –style had gone out of the CRC. Local CRC officers can only be effective if they are made to work with local voluntary organisations, but they want to take over heads of organisations and tell them what to do, in spite of the fact that the local organisations knew what the grass roots problems are, the very problems which, in the beginning, had led to the formation of the CRC. For the local organisations the problems remained the same as before there was a local CRC office.

We expected the local CRC to be in the town as watchdogs. It was to help local community groups by promoting and encouraging their efforts in education at all levels, in employment matters and in carrying their casework load. The CRC should assist them to obtain needed funds like the Urban Aid Programme and provide advice and information as an articulate centre in terms of both skills and resources.

Many of the problems we talked about in all the list of needs, the local CRC has not solved. The problems remained and we had to solve as many as we could ourselves. We did solve them. Those people who serve their local communities voluntarily should be the ones to whom government gives money to serve the people. It does not matter how many offices you set up. Once people have been served by those they know, who give service freely as their own chosen vocation, those are the ones the people trust, and they remain the ones capable of giving the required service, not the ones officialdom appoint. The CROs may not always succeed in getting the job done.

The CRC had some helpful effects. The police and others received helpful information. The police had representatives on the CRC. They would hear Mr. Chinna, of the Indian Workers' Association, speak about problems some Asians have with the law, because the Sikh may have to carry a sword and wear a turban while driving a bus or being a bus conductor. They would hear Mr. Ghuman saying that people from Pakistan who may not speak English very well, may not understand what is said when police stop them and ask for papers. The police may take them into custody and they may not understand why. Others, like the medical profession, social services, the Chamber of Commerce, the local education officer and white Church officials picked up useful information increasing their awareness of difficulties to be overcome.

The police and the schools did a lot, because of the evidence produced in the surveys, because our daily casework highlighted the need, and because of the encouragement of the CRC committee. The CRC committee does a lot of good work. The office records minutes and agenda, answers the telephone and gives out information. The influence of a Community Relations Officer varies from place to place according to their ability to work with the community organisations.

In spite of Government money being made available for the work of Community Relations the original voluntary organisations continued without financial help.

THE PRESS AND ITS DRAMATISATION

Between 1969 and 1975 the press had published varying kinds and types of stories and facts about me and my work, and about some of those who worked with me, some who were benefited and some who felt uneasy about the work we were doing and where we were going.

The main objectives of the press were to bring news and information with excitement and drama to the community, to inform them, to educate them with what is going on in the community.

I must say the newspapers did very well out of our work. They did not have to look far to see what was going on. They were looking straight at our work and sometimes standing side by side with us.

Drama was not my business. That was the concern of the newspapers. Who is going to read dead and dull stories, whether in a book or a newspaper?

I was not locked in a large office with double glazed windows, closed doors, sound proof walls, an enquiry desk, a large secretarial staff and Directors and Managers. Three women and I manned the day-to-day case work and carried out the objectives of the WRRO. Also the twelve regional representatives came to help our work in the evenings by doing various activities in the community: looking at the people's problems at home, at work, with the police, with their matrimonial and family lives, as well as running classes for adults and children to further their skills and education. This work was done in part of my own house and a shed in my back garden, in the Church Hall that we used for Church services and education, and at the houses of some of the representatives. One was the home of Geoffrey and Mary Bould. They were Quakers and Geoff. was one of the chairmen of WRRO. He would keep small meetings at his house and help a few people with some of their problems. Most of the representatives would help people from their home base as well as our main base.

The newspapers did a lot for us. *The Evening Echo, The Watford Observer, The West Herts Post* and sometimes *The Sunday Observer,* and *The Standard* and others who might pick up their stories from our, then, three local papers. Those who needed our services knew how and where to find us. They also knew what to expect. The service we gave was most appreciated by the needy. We had no set hours. People would wake us in the night to help someone or to go to the police station. People would call us to say, "I have just been arrested," or "My son/daughter has just been arrested."

One Sunday two police officers came into my Church Service as I was halfway through my sermon to ask me to come and help them. A family with three small children had just been evicted. They were in the street with their things in the pouring rain. The children were cold and wet and hungry. I turned the Service over to the Secretary and went with the police. I found shelter, clothes and food. The next day I went to the Town Clerk's office and they provided one of their compulsory purchase houses for town development, as a temporary measure until the family could be given a council house.

From 1969 to 1975 there were over 200 newspaper reports, either front page headlines or special features or some other large headline to do with me and my work. Most were helpful. Some set me up intentionally to be a target for a bit of mud slinging and threats upon my life and character. Here are some examples of the headlines:

Jamaican Realist Warning. Frankly Speaking to David Douglas; by Norman Wright.
Across the Racial Divide with Black Pentecostalism; by Brian Cooper.
No White Man Knows What It's Like To Be Black and Out Of A Job; by Martin White.
Immigrants' War On Race Demo.
Front Room Office Permit — The Result of Vulgar Pressure.
Immigrants' Leader Gets Racist Note.
Black Power is No Answer.
Hate Note Gets Sent To Leader.
Surrender Plea To Illegal Immigrants.

Don't Sign Any More Death Warrants. Immigrant Leader Appeal may Go To The Queen.
Race Chief Raps Council Over Grants.
English As You Work. Employers Who Employ Large Numbers Of Immigrants Are To Start Holding Adult Education Classes At Work As A Result Of The Survey Carried Out By The WRRO.
How To Beat Gazumping Brigade.
The New Neighbours Arrive.
Immigrants Get No Help From Their Own City.
Crash Language Course For Nurses – A Lifesaver.
In-Home Lesson Plan For Immigrants.
The New Race Watchdogs.
Migrants Claim Race Board Is Useless.
Hate Vandals Attack.
Immigration Bill and The Bible.
Immigration Bill: National Day Of Mourning.
The Black-led Churches In Britain.

I have already quoted other headlines on page 20 under the heading IN THE NEWS. I have picked out headline titles to show the good as well as weaknesses, such as looking at a headline to form a conclusion, as many people do, without gaining the background information by reading the full story and seeking out the evidence or the real truth. Newspapers are there to give facts. If the "fact" is right it will lead you to the truth. In my experience with press reporting, there has only ever been one wrong "fact" reported by a paper. The public should appreciate the press. Our ears and eyes are there to hear and see good and bad, so the media are there to report both. It is for us to see how it affects us and to do what we can about it, if something needs to be done.

RELATIVES INTERVENE

By 1972 I was receiving hate notes and death threats. Close friends and relations, brothers, sisters, cousins, were confused and anxious. They persuaded my mother to come from Jamaica, my brother from USA and my elder sister from Canada. Other relatives abroad wrote letters asking me to give up what I was doing, as I might be killed. My relations and friends kept beside me when I was at home, and elsewhere I was under the protection of members of the WRRO. One reporter, Norman Wright was so concerned that he contacted the local police who kept a constant watch on movements and developments. The Superintendent became worried on a number of occasions when meetings were arranged between myself and some anti-black-immigrants organisations. Nevertheless I had to hold these meetings to let them know we were here, and here to stay, just as people from this country go to other parts of the world and stay there; to Africa, the Caribbean, Pakistan, India.

When my mother, sister and brother arrived, they sat through the meetings of my organisation and discussed with members all the implications. Afterwards, along with a large proportion of the membership of the organisation, they issued a statement to everyone concerned about my well being. This said that they fully recognised their deep concern and anxiety about my safety. Their concern was much appreciated. However, such very necessary and valuable work must go on, come what may. God had given this leader a job to do and it must be done. God brought David here to do His will. We thank God that he is here and for enabling him to do so much with so little. It is a miracle. Since God had chosen him, we pray that God will see him through the darkest times and allow no harm to come to him, unless God decides he has come to the end of his journey. Therefore you must continue to give him your support, your love and your prayers.

My mother read the statement. Then she added, "God bless the day when he gave you the son he also gave to me. May long life be the will of God for him. God will take care of him."

CHAPTER FOUR

Working Together

"Until we all reach unity in the Faith and in the knowledge of the Son of God and become mature, attaining to the whole measure of the fullness of Christ."

The Holy Bible (NIV), Ephesians 4:13

MAKING RACE RELATIONS WORK
REACHING OUT IN FAITH TOGETHER
SEARCHING FOR RELATIONSHIPS
LEWISHAM AND LUTON
A CENTRE AT SELLY OAK

MAKING RACE RELATIONS WORK

Where and how did we begin to make Race Relations work? Instead of lodging complaints on behalf of members of the community to the Race Relations Board, who took too long to conduct an enquiry so that we rarely succeeded, we began to see employers and other agencies who may have been the alleged discriminator and talked about the complaints or grievances. Under those procedures employers were prepared to listen. Even if they did not have a Union membership within their company, they knew that in terms of Trade Union and industrial relations, you must have the right to be heard as a worker or a servant. That was what the employers wanted and they co-operated. It began to work so well that when some managements were having problems with complaints they would send for me or for Ann Paye. As we advanced, things became better and complaints became less. After 1975 until 1987 there were few complaints in Hertfordshire apart from some sections of the Social Services Departments.

The poor as a whole suffered, both black and white, and women. In a wide range of ways there was much more discrimination against blacks. The discriminator who acted out of knowledge or fear, made it look impossible to detect his or her unscrupulous methods. Both blacks and whites discriminated, but blacks had very little power to discriminate because they were not in management positions. Sooner or later they would be discriminated against by someone who had the power to do so.

Here are two examples. A small company may not refuse to employ 4 or 5 blacks in a workforce of 12 to 14 people, but they might hide the amount of pay given to the whites by saying to them, "Keep that under your hat." They would pay the blacks much lower wages and expect them to produce more work. They might promote a white worker and claim that they cannot promote the blacks because there are more whites than blacks and it will cause trouble. Perhaps the whites will not take orders from blacks.

A black person might rent a flat, but he may have to pay a higher rent than the white man and accept some extra restrictions written into the agreement.

From 1968 there were Race Relations Laws to help combat racism, but the law was weak and has certainly helped very little.

REACHING OUT IN FAITH TOGETHER

Just as we wanted industries and other areas of the life of the people to display justice and racial harmony, we wanted the same for the Churches and local congregations. Although many Ministers will tell you that all are welcome in their Churches, some Churches had many black members, few of whom would ever be given positions of skill or responsibility. How many were Ministers, Bishops, Deacons, Moderators, Priests? How many sat on Church Boards and Committees?

If I was asked to share a Service or duties in a white-led Church, I would agree. Those days we shared funerals, baptisms, Christening of children, seminars, Prayer Services, House Meetings, House to House Studies. The first Minister we worked with was the Rev. Irwin Barnes. We went to many house groups. David Hillman, Deacon and school teacher, was one of the house group leaders. **This went well and boosted the beginning of a racially integrated Christian presence, removing a cloud of fear and alienation.**

Sad as some of our funeral services were, when the people saw the Rev. Barnes and me working together **it raised their spirits to hope and cheerfulness.**

Next Cardinal Heanan, after I wrote to him and he heard about Watford, visited Watford and later sent his right-hand ambassador with special responsibility to West Indian Catholics, Father Paul Foster, O.P. of the Dominican Order. We met at St. Joseph's Church in Hemel Hempstead with the priest in charge of the Church, Father John Foster. **We ate together and talked for many hours about the work and we supported each other from that day.** My colleagues and I shared services with Father John Foster and received some financial assistance for our work. I preached at St. Joseph's. Father Paul Foster worked at Watford at all levels with us, and in London and other places. Father Paul Foster was deeply involved with the setting up of IMCGB and the campaign for Watford CRC, as well as in the Working Party that produced the book on Pastoral Care for the British Council of Churches Guide for Ecumenical Development.

Next was Father Adrian Edwards, Professor at Radlett Roman Catholic Theological College. He was of the Order of the Holy Ghost Fathers and very keen on Pentecostalism. He invited me to give talks at the College on Pentecostalism and shared in most of my Services. Some of the young men who were being trained as priests came on Sundays and taught the Sunday School in my Services. **Father Edwards always visited my home and we visited people in the parish together**. He left to teach in Nigeria. I missed him very much.

Thus we have set these patterns among the people at local levels, as an example of the task for others to do for themselves.

SEARCHING FOR RELATIONSHIPS

The black and white Churches have all done a great work together since I made the first approach to the British Council of Churches and met with the Rev. John Leake, the Secretary to the Division of Ecumenical Affairs, in the early part of 1970. That's when we began to seek Associate Membership of the BCC for IMCGB.

We have seen many pyramids and clouds of racism disappear during the time we worked and served together in concern for the better development of evangelism and sharing living and working together.

That small beginning brought Rev. Roswith Gerloff, a German Pastor of the German Lutheran Church to Britain to research into Pentecostalism and possibly to do her Doctorate*. Among others, Roswith joined me in my work in Watford in the early Spring of 1971, in the Church, WRRO, and IMCGB and immediately began to work between us and the BCC at Eaton Gate in London, and with Selly Oak College in Birmingham. I met Professor Hollenweger who wrote *The Pentecostals*** and *Pentecost between Black and White*.***

We worked at Selly Oak that year, Professor Hollenweger, Roswith, Ann Paye and myself. A number of weekend seminars were arranged by Roswith and the Professor and workshops were led by Church Leaders, such as Rev. Michael Harper of the Fountain Trust. By 1972 I was at places like the BCC Assembly and the World Council of Churches in Geneva. With Professor Hollenweger I went to Germany and Switzerland. By 1972 Rev. John Leake and other BCC staff were visiting Watford and sharing in various of our Pentecostal Convocations. Rev. Michael Elliot, who was then in charge of the Community and Race Relations Unit came to see our project and gave us the first ever financial assistance as Grant Aid for our work. We knew that the small beginning was going to grow.

I was still very cautious and doubtful as to whether the BCC would ever accept an application for the Associate Membership of the IMCGB and often spoke to John Leake about my feeling and doubt. He used to say that the BCC could not afford not to accept IMCGB's application. "Why do you think so?" I asked. "They would have too much to lose. This is the way ahead and I see already that IMCGB with your leadership is going to provide the bridge for the future." He wrote a letter to me on 22nd August 1973 in which he said, "I am interested to note that you are hoping for a decision on the application for BCC membership in September and suggest that you try to appoint a group

A Plea for British Black Theologies, Published by Peter Lang **Published by SCM Press. ***Published by Christian Journals Limited.

of three or four people, who could meet with a similar group from BCC for informal discussions. I think it would be better if you did this before pressing for a decision on application as it would ensure that any difficulties were anticipated before the final step is taken. I shall be very interested to hear the results of your meeting." That was John's last letter to me, for sadly he died not long afterwards. Although it took much longer than John and I had hoped, our application was accepted in the long run.

By now Roswith was going from England to Germany frequently, teaching and reporting the vast wealth of work and learning Pentecostalism had to offer here in Britain, as well as Germany and other parts of the world. She would write to me from Germany and we would meet and work together in Watford, in London and in Birmingham. She wrote and made recordings of our services, and wrote short pieces for radio and journals in Germany. I had enabled her to meet most of the Black Church Leaders in Britain and when she knew some of them well enough she visited their Churches to do further research. She was much loved by the black people. Roswith went to Jamaica and from there to the USA in search of further information about the history of Pentecostalism, both to find out more and to ratify what I and the other black Church leaders had told her. **By then the BCC had begun to see more clearly the great value of the work that Roswith had embarked upon and decided that they were going to support her all the way both with resources and manpower**. She was away for about eight months.

Early in 1974 Mr. Martin Conway, who had taken over the position of the late Rev. John Leake, came to see me. Five of us met in Watford. We decided to meet next time at the British Council of Churches offices at 2 Eaton Gate. That meeting was in February 1975. Rev. Sheila Douglas, Rev. Roswith Gerloff and Miss Ann Paye came with me.

Subsequently Rev. Harry Morton, Mr. Martin Conway and Rev. Elliot Kendall expressed interest in our events. We invited them to our Convocations. They were guest speakers at a big gathering at St. Saviour's Church in Hornsey.

We took every opportunity to identify the various Church Leaders and Officials at the BCC. Rev. Harry Morton gave talks on "What is the British Council of Churches?" Before those days the name BCC used to sound to black Church leaders like the crack of a whip at wild pigeons in the desert. They would fly away in fear. Now black Leaders and their members were beginning to be slightly more relaxed. Further meetings in 1975 and 1976 looked at the role of Black-led Churches, their presence, their growth, deprivation of buildings and the misconceptions of the indigenous British Churches. There was a fear of the black-led presence growing within our community as noisy groups all over the place, who seemed to some a bit eccentric. Some thought they were a breeding ground for racialism. Others felt that black Ministers were not really Ministers, but self-styled and self-ordained. They thought black Ministers would not be able to do much and that if you asked them to speak they would repeat themselves and be lost for words after about five minutes. These were some of the fears among white-led Churches. The black-led Churches made claim to healing and Holy Spirit anointing and such things. Misconceptions and myths brought fear.

It was the concern of BCC and ourselves to find common ground to educate each other and eliminate these fears. We discussed doctrine and belief to establish that the black-led Churches practising Pentecostalism according to *The Acts of the Apostles** did overwhelmingly come within the rules of acceptance laid down by the British and World Councils of Churches, and did qualify to join as *bone fide* members of BCC.

We had studied IMCGB's constitution, its objectives and articles of faith and realised that the articles of faith of Pentecostals in membership of IMCGB are acceptable to BCC members. I led the black Churches to BCC to seek support, help, participation in evangelism and sharing the work of God together as one people in one faith with different understandings. Having established both the enrichments of black-led Churches as well as the deprivations, in that black-led Churches needed places to worship and resources to run our education programmes and had difficulty in finding positive and true acceptance, I acted in hope of a better future exhibiting better understanding and true partnership.

*See *The Holy Bible*.

LEWISHAM AND LUTON

It was agreed at one of our meetings in 1976, that Martin Conway should launch a meeting to involve a much larger membership of black-led and white-led British Churches, to look at the relationships between the largely white, mainstream, historic, traditional Churches and the largely newly-established, immigrant, spiritual, often Pentecostal, Churches. That meeting was to follow up the report the BCC Assembly received in April that year of the new, black presence in Britain. The meeting was held as a 24 hour consultation on 1st and 2nd September 1976. A Consultation Draft was prepared for the meeting. Twenty seven heads of Churches out of 40 invited met at Dartmouth House, Lewisham, London. From the Consultation a small Working Party was set up to take initiatives to involve wider participation, to bring recommendations that would get white and black Church leaders working together. The Division of Ecumenical Affairs of the BCC had agreed to these proposals. The Working Party of eight was elected as follows: David Douglas (IMCGB, Bethel Apostolic Church), Ira Brooks (New Testament Church of God), Martin Conway (BCC Division of Ecumenical Affairs), S. E. Reynolds (Calvary Church of God in Christ), Herbert Sealy (Pilgrim Wesleyan Holiness Church), Moses Sephula (African Methodist Episcopal Church), Martin Simmonds (First United Church of Jesus Christ Apostolic), A. Walters (Shiloh Pentecostal Fellowship).

We decided that as many heads of Church organisations as possible should be invited to a conference to be held at one of the branches of Calvary Church of God in Christ at Dale Road, Luton, from 11a.m. to 4p.m. on 30th October 1976. The Conference would elect those people who would in future represent Pentecostalism as Members of the Joint Working Party between black-led and white-led Churches. Seventy two black-led Churches listed under the names of the Churches, with the Heads of those Churches, were invited to attend the Luton Conference with at least two representatives of each Church. These seventy two Churches were those listed black-led Churches to be published in the *World Christian Handbook 1977** onwards. These were Churches known to me as well as others, Churches that had started up in Britain since 1968. Member Churches of the BCC were represented at the Luton Conference, mostly the Church of England and the Methodist Church.

In between the Lewisham Conference in September and the Luton Conference in October many things happened. The work set up at Lewisham was becoming quite involved and planning went on with Roswith Gerloff, Martin Conway and myself. Various facts and concerns that must be known about black-led Churches, as well as various things the black-led Churches must know about BCC had been studied. The necessary work had to be done and put on paper to show the issues involved on both sides, so that future partnership could be clearly discussed. The Working Party met to consider them. As the person with the background knowledge and practising experience about black-led Churches and Community and Race Relations, I had to provide written information.

Whilst we were busy doing all these things a group of black Church leaders called a meeting at Willesden, London. Some of them came to see me in Watford. Some of them had been at all the previous meetings with us and with the various divisional representatives of the BCC and at the Luton Conference. One of these men was on the Working Party that signed the letter of Joint Accountability to the Joint Working Party Invitation to the Luton Conference. They had planned a meeting to discourage the Luton Conference. As a result, sometime later, the body called Afro-West Indian United Council of Churches (AWUCOC) was formed. It was not a member of BCC. I always insisted that a place for their representative be kept for them on any of our joint partnership working parties or committees, hoping they would study the thinking behind IMCGB and the needs our actions are designed to meet.

IMCGB was the first ever black initiative Christian Council of Churches in the United Kingdom.

*The section on the United Kingdom includes comprehensive statistical and descriptive data on the black-led Churches by Roswith Gerloff.

Since its inception three or four others have come into being, three of which had rivalry in them and two showed rivalry to IMCGB and BCC. Competition is good if it delivers the goods, that is, that all councils should work to help co-operation and sharing resources and skills and be seen working shoulder to shoulder with the white-led Churches in Britain, as IMCGB has done since we commenced at the end of the 60s.

At Luton fifteen representatives of black-led Churches were elected to the Conference of the Joint Working Party between black and white. **They were to explore ways ahead to establish the presence of black and white Christians working together and sharing resources and faith, with a common hope of spreading the Gospel, irrespective of the colour of their leader's skin or the colour of the people we serve. If we believe Christ, then we must be of the same household of faith in practice.** The 15 people were those elected at Lewisham with others in addition. Towards the end of 1976 and early in 1977 we planned and met and visited Churches round the country. In April 1977 I placed heavy emphasis on the need to provide training for black Pastors and lay people in the black Pentecostal Churches as well as others, as I pointed out in an article in *Renewal**.

*See *Renewal*, February and March 1977, p12, "Love and Equality Across Barriers".

A CENTRE AT SELLY OAK

Martin Conway and Rev. Dick Wooton invited some members of the Working Party to a lunch meeting to plan a meeting in July1977 about what Partnership will now be doing for the way ahead. We met on 19th April and made firm proposals. Education in Theology and the setting up of an Advice and Information Centre were taken up as high priority needs facing Partnership. Dr. Walter Hollenweger, Professor of Mission, proposed a small beginning for Theological study for black Church Leaders and Pastors of the Partnership, as a pilot project to permit interchange. The Joint Working Party met at Harborne Hall, Selly Oak Colleges, Birmingham, on 15th and 16th July 1977 with members of the Division of Ecumenical Affairs of the BCC. These included the Bishop of Willesden, the Rt. Rev. Hewlett Thomson, Rev. Colin Scott, later Bishop of Manchester, Rev. Victor Watson and Rev. Dick Wooton. The Bishop of Willesden was asked to be chairman. This two day consultation agreed to a small beginning with Theological Education, provided money could be raised to support the cost. A future agenda was agreed. The programme was as follows: 1. Housing the Centre; 2. Produce a revised list of contact persons and member Churches; 3. Further material on education; 4. Sharing experiences in local contacts; 5. Raise genuine questions that must be faced between us; 6. Discuss the whole matter of membership in local Councils of Churches; 7. The booklet, *Partnership between Black and White,* by Roswith Gerloff.

Martin Conway was asked to write to the German Lutheran Church to ask for a further extension for Roswith Gerloff to be absent from her duties in Germany, to continue the great work ahead of us in Partnership between Black and White, for which she had already done so much, so well. That meant that we would have to employ her, if the German Headquarters agreed, and if the BCC and other bodies of the BCC and German Churches would help to finance the work which would continue on a wider basis. The German Churches agreed, and so did the BCC and member Churches and organisations. We spent the rest of 1977 planning and preparing.

Great strides had been taken and these were featured at BCC Assemblies in Spring and Autumn 1978 at Birmingham and Nottingham, and at WCC. The BCC Assembly accepted the plan for a

Centre with staff, with Roswith Gerloff as Director and Martin Simmonds as Co-Director, and a Secretary. The Centre for Black and White Christian Partnership is now* fully in swing. The Course for the Certificate in Theology began in 1978 with an Information and Advice Centre that served Great Britain, Europe and other parts of the world. We had a Management Committee and an Education Committee, which included the Bishop of Dudley, Rt. Rev. Tony Draper, Bishop Malachi Ramsay (later to become IMCGB's First Pentecostal Archbishop) and Rev. Moses Sephula. Now we had most of our meetings in Birmingham round that Education Centre, and planned further useful projects of development, fundraising, advertisement and publications. During 1979 our first celebration with songs of praises, involved students and others from various parts of the world who had met us and become involved. They wanted to share and take with them the spirit of Partnership. Meanwhile we had to pursue the daily task in the venture of exchange and support in various towns and districts throughout the United Kingdom. We were looking for a way ahead towards the end of 1979 and throughout 1980, to wean Partnership to work as a unit with a wider supporting body. On 11th October 1980 a meeting was held at St. Matthews Meeting Place in Brixton, London, where the old Joint Working Party presented reports and recommendations and was to set up a new supporting body. Three reports were prepared, one presented by Rev. Moses Sephula, one by Mr. Martin Conway and one by me, Rev. David Douglas.

As a result, the Conference for Christian Partnership (CCP) was set up, with terms of reference to support the life of the Church through sharing of faith and resources, through helping to educate and teach and in places to co-ordinate support and joint evangelism.

Rev. Vic. Watson and Rev. Io Smith were elected co-chairmen. The Rev. Colin Davey succeeded Martin Conway at BCC and continued his excellent work with CCP from within the Division of Ecumenical Affairs. The CCP has been in many large towns in the United Kingdom, to meet workers and share problems and bring hope and joy.

*i.e. in 1992

I was glad I had struggled up those winding stairs of the BCC that cold, dark day in 1969 and 1970 and from then on. I had told John Leake at that time that I had come to seek help and support to spread the Gospel and to share the spirit of alleviating deprivation in the community. I had told him how it felt in a new land when we were not acknowledged by our brothers in Christ, and even more, when our faith and suffering did not seem to matter to them.

CHAPTER FIVE

Grass Roots and Government

"I have heard all about you, Lord, and am filled with awe by the amazing things you have done. In this time of our deep need, begin again to help us, as you did in years gone by. Show us your power to save us. And in your anger, remember your mercy."

The Holy Bible (NLT), Habakkuk 3:2

BACK IN THE SOCIAL SECTOR OF MY OWN CHURCH PRACTICE
FACTORS OF CONCERN
HEAD AND HEART
THE ACTS OF THE APOSTLES

BACK IN THE SOCIAL SECTOR OF MY OWN CHURCH PRACTICE

The Bethel Apostolic Church has been running projects in parts of London for many years in Supplementary Education and Training as well as literacy education for adults, as we have done in Watford and elsewhere. Brixton and Islington, in particular, had very bad conditions. In both boroughs some of our Church members' children were having serious problems, some with schools, some with petty crimes, drugs and difficulty in finding jobs as school leavers. It was 1978 and we had been working in Church Services since 1959, running projects just from the Church resources since 1975. It was time for me to take up the advice, in the reply dated 4th May 1972 to my letter to the Prime Minister, that a new programme for Urban Aid* was to be announced. Attached to that reply were Guidelines and information of the Local Act 1969 on Grants for Social Needs.

So, in 1978, a working Social Need Department was set up by the Church, giving membership to non-Church members who could in some ways assist the Church welfare work in the local and wider communities. This body consisted of Church members from many parts of London and the Home Counties. The Church is the Charity and the Mother organisation. The local needs of the people would be met by funds and Grant Aid given through the local Council by central government, provided that funds applied for specifically to meet the needs in Brixton, Lambeth, would be used only for Brixton. The body named the United Church Welfare and Workers' Association (UCWWA), was set up, and constituted as a nationwide department of the Church, run and managed by heads of the Churches, with a local Management Committee. We made our first application under section 71 of the 1969 Provision for Social Needs in the Local Government Programme. We were the first to do that as a black-leadership Church and voluntary organisation running such services in Lambeth. We operated a Mechanical Engineering Workshop from an old garage, music, art and office-work training from Hayter Road, and Supplementary Education from St. Matthews Meeting Place. We had a paid staff looking after the day-to-day overall running of the project: 13 class teachers, 7 of whom were trained, 4 were highly trained and there

*See p. 40

were two students from Polytechnic who would be on placement for a period. We had a full Advice Service with a number of Law experts and other specialists giving up their time to serve people with problems.

In 1979 we made our first application for Urban Aid through Lambeth Council. We received our first payment of grants through Lambeth Department of the Environment (DOE) and Inner City Partnership (ICP) in 1979: a grant of £23,000 revenue towards running costs and salaries. We had to find the remaining amount of monies from the Churches, British Council of Churches, World Council of Churches (WCC), Inner London Education Authority (ILEA), Silver Jubilee Trust, the Methodist Church and personal donations. Even so that was not enough. We needed a premises that could accommodate the whole volume of work. We received £32,750 as Capital Grant by Partnership Urban Aid towards the purchasing or leasing of a premises. The Council was to find us a suitable building. We looked at many that the District Valuer had. They were derelict. The £32,750 could not buy a flat in Lambeth, much less a building that served many projects that catered for hundreds of people daily. At one time we went to see one of these buildings in Clapham. My colleague fell through the roof and landed in a pile of rubble and muck. We had to send for help with rope and ladder to get him out. We had to crawl on hands and knees with masks and trench lights and ladder to reach him.

In 1981, 42 Clapham Manor Street, a Grade Two listed building, a large building on a large site, built in the eighteenth century, was available for us to see. The building had great potential for the work we do, but it would cost a fortune to make habitable. However, as a listed building of public heritage and value, I was prepared to move mountains to restore it to accommodate such an important project that meant so much to the deprived people of Lambeth. I decided that we should seek approval from Lambeth Council for four things: 1. To be prepared to lease the property; 2. To ask them for more money for staff and other revenue costs; 3. To ask them for more capital for work to be carried out on the premises; 4. Planning and time to carry out the work before the lease was to be signed by the Church (UCWWA). Lambeth agreed to all except the providing of more money to refurbish the building. We approached the DOE and got £20,000 with the support of the ICP Grant Officer. The architect and the surveyors estimated that the £50,750 we now had to carry out the work was probably just enough to cover the cost of materials. We had no money for labour and other costs and Lambeth Council would not move an inch to help with building finance.

I contacted the Rt. Hon. James Prior, Minister for the Department of Employment on 20th June 1981. He invited me to discuss the matter with Lord Gowrie. On 30th July 1981 Rev. V. Watson and Rev. Ken Douglas, acting as my deputies, met Lord Gowrie. They discussed our project: Education, Employment, Training, Advice Centre, Arts and Crafts; all the things in which we were engaged in our ongoing project. We discussed the cost of refurbishing 42 Clapham Manor Street, by the only way we could devise, which was as a training measure under a Manpower Services Commission (MSC) Community Training Programme. Arrangements were made for me to see Mr. Finnimore, Head of Community Programmes at the time.

Soon our application was in and the grant was approved. The work commenced in 1982 with 57 men and women and 15 Supervisors and Managers. The turnover, as far as I was concerned, was good. It went up to 120 men and women in training per month. But the work was not up to standard, being done by trainees, not by skilled workers, and, the building being a listed building, things had to be replaced bit by bit, reconstructing some parts exactly as they had been in the 18th century. The other setback was that the entire drainage system had to be replaced at a cost of £70,000 for materials more than was estimated at first. We also built a new workshop which is separate from the main building, and we added new dressing and washing rooms, bathrooms and toilets that could cater for large numbers of people daily including handicapped and disabled people and small children. The MSC Community Programme scheme went as far as it could with the type of skill the workers had, and with all sorts of new discoveries of new setbacks found. The training programme brought the building up to the stage where it was habitable and looked very nice, but was not finished. The programme ended in 1984.

We approached Lambeth Council again to ask for the money to complete the building, to meet the various statutory regulations and to put in all the special architectural features. Lambeth advised us to have it surveyed and costed. We did, and the estimated cost was £185,500.

This estimate I discussed with Council officials and the bid was put forward in Spring 1985 for the DOE under the same Urban Aid programme to provide this sum. Otherwise we would not be able to continue in the building as it failed the statutory environmental requirements. Because of the recognition, respect and value placed on the work we had done, we were able to carry out some of our functions with certain limitations. We restricted numbers, with no more than a few hundred on the premises at any one time. The handicapped and disabled were not to be included until completion, and no heavy mechanical machinery should be permanently used until after completion.

We were able to hold a Supplementary School for children having difficulty with school work, attendance and behaviour. Mr. Victor Anfu, a qualified and experienced teacher and an officer in Divine Healing Church, Kilburn, where I am Leader, was in charge of this Project, which included school liaison as well as the children's learning. A number of teachers and other helpers were employed.

When we checked with the DOE in early summer 1985, they told me they were waiting for a letter from the ICP signed by the head of ICP as well as one from the District Valuer's Department. When I checked with the Community Grants Officer of ICP, he had not had time to get round to it yet. Months later I asked the District Valuers if this matter had been discussed with them, and they said, "No!" I got onto Inner City Partnership again and advised that I had spoken with the District Valuers and asked them to write the necessary letter so that the District Valuer could sign the document required by the DOE. After that, the only thing we heard was that someone was away, or on holiday, or sick.

Everything in Lambeth was upside down. About thirty Councillors were threatened with disqualification from office. We felt all hope was destroyed. We received a letter from the head of ICP, as well as from the leader of Lambeth Council, stating that funds would end on 31st July and that we were required to hand over the building and all assets to them. We argued the case. We had been established in the community since 1978. Many members of the community were dependent on our project. Already we had spent on the building £235,500 and we could not give up at that stage. Besides, there was also a new building, the mechanics workshop, built with Government money, by the Church for the Church's project, but on Lambeth's land.

We continued the project at 42 Clapham Manor Street until January 2nd 1987. That was as long as the Church's money would allow. God, in his mercy, kept us there until then. We finished our Christmas Holiday Project, said goodbye to the children and got ready to hand over the keys to Lambeth. The final letter to accompany the handing over of the keys was written.

We removed our project from Lambeth to Kilburn and continued at Watford and Kilburn doing what we could for the people of Lambeth.

We placed in writing our position with regard to the equipment and the building on which we had spent so much money, both money from central Government and our own money. We expected the building to be completed and that the separate workshop should be returned to us to carry out our work. We expected that Lambeth would work out ways to remedy the damage done by their decision to withdraw funding and the building from us, but we were disappointed.

The UCWWA has become part of IMCGB and will continue the work it was set up to do in as many parts of this country as possible. We do these things for the spreading of the Gospel and sharing our experiences with the deprived.

If everyone felt this way, everyone in Lambeth would have a job and a proper home to live in. There would be fewer crimes. The streets of Lambeth would be safe. We believe these things could come about if we try in obedience to God.

One of the great achievements of the UCWWA in Lambeth was to remedy the underachievement of children in secondary school. We taught these children, let them sit exams at our level, based on their school lessons and subjects. We made sure they were ready and able to cope with exams at their regular Council or ILEA or other type school.

Parents found that their children made tremendous progress after coming to our school at "Clapham Manor". Another good thing was that many parents came to our school with their children. Some of those children went out of their way to prove to their parents that they were willing to do good work. Parents were able to understand better what school was all about in a new technological age. They were able to use the computer workshop and practice art, craft, music, drama, role play and looking after one another. One of the most powerful methods of learning was when we got the parents to be the children and the children to be the parents. This was done in a real work setting.

Apart from the vast learning success, such training built a level of understanding and co-operation at home between parents and children. This had improved behaviour generally.

An anti-social behaviour pattern is found in children who live in such deprived places as Brixton, with a high crime rate. From our practice, relationships improved at school and other places where those children went. These changes were seen by parents, relations, teachers and other people in the community.

FACTORS OF CONCERN

We have been doing this spiritual and social work of the Church in Britain for thirty years now. Britain is heaven for the rich, the powerful, the privileged and the well-favoured, but difficult for others who are poor and deprived. Third world countries often get better help and attention from us in Britain than our own poor. Here the poor are often brushed aside by bureaucrats to become a sure, permanent feature within this rich and plenteous land.

The poor remain with us. They would not be so sorrowful if they had a reasonable house to live in, could afford proper food and keep warm during wintertime. The unemployed with young children and the elderly and infirm suffer most. We seriously believe better can be done. That must come from those who hold power. Governments must be committed to meeting the needs of the people: housing, health care, education, employment, crime, poverty. Some of us like the challenge and cut and thrust of opposition from time to time, but not when we are hungry, unemployed, homeless and being mugged, raped or beaten up, shot or knifed in the streets or at home. Deprivation is a major contributor to social disorders and crime.

New blood came to the House of Commons. Four new black MPs were elected for the Labour Party in the June 1987 General Election. They brought for discussion and action, from their own grass roots experience, the needs of those in this community who are seriously deprived, a vast proportion of whom are black. However dark it is for the white British poor, it is much darker for the blacks.

WRRO set up an anti-drugs campaign to assist those who take highly dangerous addictive drugs, and discourage alcoholism, smoking and other excesses. Sometimes we were snubbed or fobbed off by politicians and "experts". We were told about freedom of speech and human rights for people to do what they want with their lives. Encouragement was given to people under age that it was their right to play with sex, to have a pint, and so on. Now everybody is panicking when it is too late to pick up the pieces, to reduce the immorality and make good so many wrongs. People like ourselves do not play games with other people's lives. We learn to see ahead. We would like governments to support people like us. It is the Mother Theresas who come to the rescue, the Oxfams, the people of Christian Aid, the poorer Churches, the Dr. Barnardos ... who pick up the pieces.

The problems of this country, other countries and developing countries would be far less if governments followed our lead. For example, if the teaching of the Pentecostal Churches, the Free Churches and most Anglican Churches and others had been followed, HIV/Aids would have been far less prevalent in society because of the strict doctrinal emphasis against promiscuity. That is our expected standard. It conflicts with the general consensus of politics and media presentation. It makes us in the Church ask, "Who is in charge? Who should really be in charge?" It has to be, in the end, whoever can turn around society again to abide by the standards set by Christian teaching with regard to human caring and concern. Those standards have been set aside, those rules broken. The breaking of those rules has brought fatal consequences upon the community as a whole.

HEAD AND HEART

No system that cares for human beings can afford to lose either its head or its heart. Bureaucracy has no heart. It has a big head and there is no heart to influence what it thinks.

The history of man in caring is based upon a woman and a man. It represents a bond of unity and support, a unique team, pooling the head and heart skills of each to produce the policy and practice of family life. The higher responsibility is given to the man. He has to labour and sweat for bread. That is also one part of his caring role. The role of the woman is to give care to both that labouring head and to the children she bears. The man also cares for the woman. This is the family system upon which a well-ordered society must be based if it is to flourish.

Society's provision for the welfare of its people in community needs team work between government and Church, each bringing to the exercise its own combination of head and heart.

This may give us a wide spectrum of combinations of the two, ranging from Nietzsche's godless

Superman, who advances his own cause by trampling on the weak, to the reflection, imperfectly in practice, of the perfection of reason hand in hand with compassion, originating in and exemplified in God.

If the world is to take a turn for the better, the Government and the Church are going to have to work together as head and heart. There is truth in the implications of a question asked by Bishop Desmond Tutu of South Africa. "To those who say the Church should not engage in politics, I ask, 'Which Bible do you read?'"

My analysis of Bishop Tutu's question is that the Church does not have to get involved in party politics, but it has to get involved in what the Government is doing. The Government has to respond to the head/heart input of the Church, to develop the caring role and fulfil the responsibilities of each team member to mankind, to make the law effective and pursue justice.

THE ACTS OF THE APOSTLES

We expect to see government agencies, who are there to help to meet people's needs, do just that, or else give the Church the level of resources for that purpose and look to the Church to administer this sort of care and service to the community as a whole.

In the *Acts of the Apostles** chapter 6 the Church set up a department to look after the needy, the elderly and the widows.

That is why Pentecostal Churches try so hard to stretch themselves to do caring and social work of all kinds in the community. Even if some Churches are very poor, they do the best they can because they believe this expresses the outcome of the Gospel, Christianity, the Church and Pentecostalism. That is why my Church set up WRRO, IMCGB and UCWWA as the part of the doctrine of Pentecostalism begun in *Acts* 6. They preached and taught and cared for people and I do not think we can do differently, if we want to be true Christians.

The inner experience of the mysteries of the Spirit of God has shown us that in this we do not live in vain. People who are in love with each other, as man and woman, may give us a vague idea of what this experience of God is like. It is the essence of intimacy, which is the intermingling of

*See *The Holy Bible*

both souls together in peace of mind, trust, admiration and co-ordination. When these persons will be away from each other each will think of the other and be part of the other, and by faith, trust and hope, abide. That is the nearest example I can give to illustrate the experience of the born-again Christian. It is something every man or woman will have to experience for themselves; abiding in God, giving all to Him and His will, and He, by His Spirit, coming to us, and keeping on coming, to give us reassurance that he is with us.

*The First Pentecostal Archbishop
Archbishop Malachi Ramsay*

IMCGB Historian, The late Rev. Dr. Roswith Gerloff

The late Rt. Rev. Vic. Watson, MBE, BD wearing his IMCGB Councillor's Medallion on the occasion to recognize his retirement as President of IMCGB in November 2002

Opening the IMCGB office. Rev. George Assibey, assisted by Gabriel Gibogwe, hands the keys to Rt. Rev. S. Douglas, International Moderator.

*IMCGB Ministries of Excellence Conference 2005
Church Managenment 2 Workshop.*

An IMCGB Ordination Service.

Annual General Meeting 2006, Voting

Annual General Meeting 2006, Questions and discussions

Annual General Meeting 2006
Rt. Rev. Onye Obika, Secretary General, signs the register.

The Consecration of Rt. Rev. Donnett Thomas, 17th November 2007

Rt. Rev. Onye Obika, Rt. Rev. Sheila Douglas, Rt. Rev. Colin Maloney, Rt. Rev. Donnett Thomas, Rev. Alison Trehewy
The Apostolic Team 2008

CHAPTER SIX

Making a Way Forward

"The nations will see your righteousness and all kings your glory; You will be called by a new name that the mouth of the Lord will bestow. You will be a crown of splendour in the Lord's hand, a royal diadem in the hand of your God."

The Holy Bible (NIV), Isaiah 62:2-3

A UNITING BODY FOR CHURCHES
IMCGB's INTEREST IN LEADERSHIP
UNDERACHIEVEMENT
A STRUCTURE TO FACELIFT LEADERSHIP
A PROPER BLACK INITIATIVE
ARCHBISHOP-ELECT
THE WILL OF GOD
INAUGURATION OF THE FIRST PENTECOSTAL ARCHBISHOP

A UNITING BODY FOR CHURCHES

The International Ministerial Council of Great Britain was set up as the Ecumenical Department of the Watford Bethel Apostolic Pentecostal Church, but later the department became the dominant organisation. The member Churches and their Ministers and other Church Officers play a consistent and very active working part in the life of the Council and in its long and hard efforts to bring unity between some Pentecostals and non-Pentecostal Christians and Church organisations.

Building a proper work – that is, building a local Church -- demands hard work, self-sacrifice, skill and vision, as a Church leader. IMCGB trains Church Leaders and offers a forum for discussion of the issues with which Leaders are faced.

Similarly with wider Church matters. IMCGB set out to be a uniting body, uniting black-led Churches and working in partnership with long-established white-led Churches. Now we share Church buildings, worship together and meet to plan on equal terms. It has been a long journey. We have moved towards it patiently step by step, and it is not completed yet.

The use of Church buildings was a matter that concerned us. In England many large Church buildings have very few people worshipping in them on Sunday mornings. At the same time a group with a larger membership has no Church building to meet in. A branch of the Pentecostal Church which I lead meets in a Church building in Kilburn on Sundays. Sunday is always a nervous day for me because we have to get the entire programme of that Church fitted in between 2p.m. and 5p.m. We start with Bible Study and Sunday school. Then there is the Devotional Service, Reading, Song Service, Testimony, Offering, Sermon, Announcements, Holy Communion, Special Prayers, prayers for the sick and others who come forward. After the Service many members want to talk and ask advice, or prayer. Should I tell them I can't because our time is up? When a Church building is shared the other party must understand and care about both sides of interests and not count time too much. At a time when the Church would otherwise be standing empty the host Church should not count the extra time the group spends on worship or pastoral care, neither should they charge a rent that the guest Church cannot afford.

The IMCGB raised these questions, highlighting part of the very wide divide that can be found among Christians. The question of sharing the use of Church buildings was broadly discussed through the BCC and the Sharing of Church Buildings Act was passed in 1969. The implementation of this Act, however, requires considerable co-operation and goodwill, if those who have no building can confidently find an arrangement that meets their needs.

Many discussions and consultations have taken place. The next is scheduled for January 1993 to consider reports by Rev. Onyuku and myself of difficulties experienced, and to point the way forward.

IMCGB'S INTEREST IN LEADERSHIP

Leaders of IMCGB Churches support each other through the Council, but the Council does not interfere in the internal governance of member Churches. It maintains that if the Leader of the Church supports the Council, it is up to that Leader to prepare the membership of his Church to follow, using the skilled support and service of the Council. It provides the benefit of training people for the Ministry, with a standard of prestige that was never thought of or seen accorded to Pentecostal Leaders in any past history of Pentecostalism in any part of the world. Fifteen or twenty years ago Pentecostal Church groups and their Leaders were seen as fanatics. Pentecostalism was called a sect. Their leaders and pastors held no title of recognition in England or elsewhere, either by the so-called established Churches or by the State. Now they have proper titles of recognition, by both State and Church, because IMCGB has worked hard for this acceptance by building together a trust that was necessary to provide the support and confidence required to achieve these substantial advances. This can be abused and has been. We have, however, the opportunity and machinery to deal with matters to make improvements in the course of the daily workload.

At present we have a system of selection of candidates to train for the Ministry, a method of deciding how and when they should be officially ordained, and a method of directing them towards the particular ministry for which they are best suited and can best serve. A person may not necessarily be ordained as a head Minister or become a Bishop or the Archbishop, but he/she would be ordained to the Ministry of his/her calling: Steward, Mother, Deacon, Evangelist, Pastor, Superintendent, Overseer, Elder, Minister. We, as a Council, provide a proper structure of accountability. These titles are now accepted and official, as for any other Church throughout the world. I will, however, make it clear that until a person meets the full requirements of the selection process of IMCGB, the council would not pass that person's credentials. That may not mean that the person may not be good for the Ministry, but the Council feel we must set a standard against abuse, and that the Church must be properly represented seeing the reservations that until recently existed.

In earlier years some Church people and leaders used fancy titles for themselves because they felt they had to do that to impress others. I have never known this practice to be followed by the Caribbean Pentecostals, because they have always had a simple system of leadership selection; selection of Pastors and Leaders by the people. Above that, selection of higher titles came from the USA. Here in the United Kingdom a Pastor would be ordained as a Minister or Bishop by going to the USA to have it done, or the Bishop would come from the USA. That status, however, had no value in the UK, not being recognised by Church or State, and certainly not by the USA so-called established Churches.

Now we have achieved acceptance in the UK, if it is done by the constitutional process we have set out. No-one need go around pretending with posh titles. Represent the Church with straightforward integrity, and you will receive the hospitality of the Body of Christ. If you have placed yourself under our jurisdiction and are challenged, we will account for you at the level of credible Christian Leaders.

It is important that Leaders are properly screened and elected by a people who have a registered Church organisation and are responsible to a reputable Church organisation both in terms of doctrine and the rules of the Church, and that they are practising accordingly to support the aims of the Christian Faith.

Another focus on the Leadership question arose from our determination to make use of radio broadcasting. In 1982 IMCGB first approached the Government about religious radio broadcasting. Some members of other Church organisations were extremely discouraging. I had letters telling us it would never be possible. The Government, they said, would not even consider a religious radio station. We proceeded to make a preliminary application in the early part of 1983, although the Government had not even thought of it at that point. Some Church organisations told me that, even if we could get a radio broadcasting licence, it would cost so much that we would not be able to afford it. Some MPs raised the matter in the House of Commons and a Working Party was set up to provide the Government with necessary guidelines, so that the Government could look at the possibility of Community Radio.

When this matter was made public, the Government was flooded with applications for licences for Community Radio Stations. There were to be six Community Radio Stations allowed at the first attempt. The Government abandoned the idea for a time because of certain problems which had crept in. Some of the people who had at first discouraged us were among those in the long queue of applicants for licences. The Government revitalised its intention to introduce Community Radio and we hoped the IMCGB would be able to secure a licence for the London Inter-Church Broadcasting Station, with freedom to provide for the Community as set out by the IMCGB and to meet the criteria of the Government as well as to prove an asset to the lives of the people.

In a country of wide and varying beliefs, the black-led Churches and their Church organisation and the faith of

black people need to be looked at in their worldwide setting.

I introduced a private member's proposal at the BCC, which generated much discussion in BCC and Churches Together in Britain and Ireland (CTBI)* but it was not taken forward.

My idea for a Christian Radio Station was not that it would be the prerogative of only those with money to have a voice, but it would be a resource for all practising Ministers to join in discussion of the issues of the day as they affect a Minister's work.

UNDERACHIEVEMENT

A question which arises out of this scrutiny is: Why is the largest section of the human race always at the bottom of most things? In Europe black people seem to fight against one another in most things and in Africa the same. In the Caribbean they live more acceptingly with one another until they come to Europe. West Indians and Africans in the community prefer to be led by someone else and not by a member of their own grouping, unless that leader is powerful and ruthless enough to own, enslave or totally control their lives. They do not easily accept a leader on a merely soft, Christian, democratic, peaceful and caring level. One person will have a mechanics shop or a Food Store. Many others will too. Everybody is on the same level or in the same line, and that is acceptable. If you try to take a leadership role in a calm, democratic way, you will be lonely. You are unlikely to impress your black kinsmen or to get respect and support.

*The ecumenical body that took the place of BCC in 1990.

The IMCGB has taken account of the under-achievement of the black world and knows its pitfalls. Those pitfalls will end when the black people either provide leadership from other communities who will lead to meet the needs of the black people, or else black people will have to provide and support sound leadership from their own communities. But to continue setting up one black person or group to rival another proves nothing and prevents progress. Many people like Office and honour, but few will do the work that belongs to that Office.

We will have success in real terms only by hard work of a high standard combined with professional integrity. The IMCGB has made a small beginning, has got some work done and has found a lot of answers. Our working together with the BCC, has opened a lot of closed doors and I see a very good future in the relationship of building together. Much has been accomplished in the years of the partnership and building bridges. IMCGB will continue to encourage and empower black leadership by due constitutional process to ensure the highest standards in Ministry, creating trust so that black and white can work as equal partners.

A STRUCTURE TO FACELIFT LEADERSHIP

IMCGB recognises the fear of black people about having a hierarchical structure from among them, put there by them. This fear is inherited from slavery. In the minds of black people, to be in power means to oppress and deprive. The evidence from the black political leaders of the world seems to bear out this thinking and fear. Those who seek leadership within the white-dominated structures may not be trusted.

People seem to think that a simple structure, where everybody does their own thing, is best. That is why, in the real high places of power in life, they never have a say.

The IMCGB is the planning power box of the general part of our work. In Church, community work, race relations, education, charity, leadership, organisation and strategic force, it discovers and plans ways ahead round a simple body. At the same time it cares for people. It discovers people. It treats people with dignity to make them even better. The Leadership in all these departments is the same. We honour people for long Christian service and for their determination to help make a better world. We do not honour them for being money-makers, but for what their service means to humanity.

The Council is made up of committees and departments*. It has a President, Moderator and Secretary General, Trustees and Adjudicators. It elects its own Councillors. A Councillor is a position of honour in recognition of work done in a field of service, a position given to one of knowledge, experience and understanding, who can be expected to help, guide, represent and advise the Council on matters of importance. The following persons were elected Councillors in 1983: Councillor Paul Boateng, subsequently the Rt. Hon. Paul Boateng having been elected a member of Parliament in June 1987; Councillor Sam King, then Lord Mayor of Southwark, Rev. Councillor Vic. Watson, Methodist Minister and Superintendent, later awarded the MBE, who became a Bishop of IMCGB and its President; and Councillor Sybil Phoenix, MBE, Methodist lay-preacher and Community Worker specialising in Racism Awareness Workshops**. All Councillors receive the Medallion of Honour in recognition of their service to humanity. The following received the Medallion of Honour for long, faithful and valuable contributions of service to the work of IMCGB, done voluntarily for the organisation and the betterment of mankind and the spreading of the Gospel: Miss Ann Paye and Mrs. Myrtle Dixon.

*See pp 153-154 for the management diagram as at 2007   **Working with MELRAW, a racism awareness organisation of the Methodist Church.

In seeking to promote, stimulate and acclimatise the people toward a proper leadership structure, and to get them off the see-saw of uncertainty where two sitting at either end are the same weight so they cannot come down, we have researched for five years how we could find a structure for black people and organisations which they could see as workable and sound. We hope that black people will use this example to gain their anxiously awaited desire for equality and equal opportunity. Equality means trust and respect. How can one give respect to people who have to have everything done for them, who cannot simply organise and get on together and provide something together that other people may see and want to share?

The black people will no longer have to go and share as receivers from the white people, but the white sometimes will want to come and share what the black people have to give. How will they get this kind of equality?

A PROPER BLACK INITIATIVE

That was the great triumph recognised by Councillor Sam King when he and others, three black people and one white, were awarded the Medallions of Honour as Councillors of IMCGB. He realised that black people had an organisation of their own, by means of which they could honour, not only other black men and women, but also men and women of the white community. By means of this organisation, they could give as well as receive. They were no longer crying for help, but able to take the lead. As Councillor King shouted, "We have crossed the Red Sea! We are on our way to the Promised Land!"* we acknowledged our place among the people of God journeying towards true nationhood.

*Reference to the Exodus, when Moses led the Children of Israel across the Red Sea at the beginning of their journey to the Promised Land. See *Exodus* 14:29-31 in *The Holy Bible*.

We began that journey in 1958 with the five years of special research to create the most simple organisation which would nevertheless carry the widest support. In time it must mean the first real step to a proper black initiative: within the scattered fragments establishing a framework of the wider outlook. Among the more conservative black Pentecostal Christian Church Leaders and their membership we researched and found that it is necessary to seek the support of the members to elect the First Pentecostal Archbishop.

A Pentecostal Archbishop has nothing to do with the Crown or the House of Lords, is not part of the Church of England or the Roman Catholic Church, whose heads are the Archbishop of Canterbury and the Pope. We looked for their support for our Pentecostal Archbishop, for we have always respected them. We wrote to the Archbishop of Canterbury about our intention in a letter dated 1st August 1985. We reminded him briefly of our history and work in uniting and sharing as follows:

"The International Ministerial Council of Great Britain is an Associate Member of the British Council of Churches. One of its roles is to provide ground for co-operation and working together. We have managed, over 16 years, for example, to bring Churches together to work closely with BCC, and are responsible for bringing about such things as Partnership between Black and White, The Council for Christian Partnership, the Centre for Black and White Christian Partnership at Selly Oak Colleges, Birmingham, and Theological Education presently in being at Goldsmiths' College, London."

We asked him to discuss our intention with Her Majesty the Queen if he thought it was a matter to be so raised. We received the following reply, dated 20th August 1985, from the Rev. Canon Christopher Hill, the Archbishop's Assistant for Ecumenical Affairs.

"His Grace, the Archbishop of Canterbury is at present away from Lambeth, but I know he will give very careful attention to your letter and its interesting suggestion. This may not be before the end of September, as the

Archbishop will be paying a pastoral visit to the Anglican Church in Canada at the end of this month.

"My own instinct is that it would be helpful to discuss this proposal with a group of Anglican theologians, as it could be a very important break-through in relations between black-led and Pentecostal and other Churches in this country."

Equality and sharing was beginning to look so real. For the first time we seemed to be living in a place that looked like the real world, even if it was just a small corner of the world, the Christian corner.

Some black Christians still said we were mad to think we could elect a Pentecostal Archbishop. They have always said things cannot be done. Our question is: Will they soon be electing an Archbishop too? Let us follow a structure of prestige, dignity and pride, with respect and support. With wisdom to stand in partnership to work for the success of the United Kingdom and humanity as a whole. In 1985 Heads and departments of every known black-led Church organisation were invited to give their support, or written objection if they desired to do so, for the election of an Archbishop, and later further public notice was served in *The London Gazette* of 12th June 1986.

We had applications for nomination for the office of Archbishop from Church organisations, and some for regional Bishops and Adjudicators. IMCGB's first regional bishop was Rev. J. P. Hackman*. The office of Moderator is the most skilful and sophisticated office of all, and has to be held by a person who knows and is able to work and operate every other post of the organisational duties, including the work of the pulpit. The Moderator is chosen by the Council. The Archbishop and Bishops must be nominated by their own Church organisation and then by the support of other Church Leaders and their congregations. This support has to be in writing. After each Church organisation has made its nomination, the numbers of people supporting from each and the number against has to be documented. So far we had nothing written.against a nominee or against the election of an Archbishop. A

*Editor's note: J. P. Hackman is no longer with IMCGB

few people, however, made one or two comments that they thought that sort of thing came from a white tradition. My argument is that wherever it came from, it is good, and we want what is good. Black and white should serve people from the same level, as people together.

One of the paramount reasons why the IMCGB sees it a very proper and well judged necessity to have a Pentecostal Archbishop is the need to have such a source and channel of black leadership through whom to direct co-operation at all levels of the Church's life and duty among all mankind, both believers and non-believers. That was not quite the situation until then in the social, Christian or religious movements as they stood. The black politician will not and cannot perform this function, because he is not the master of the present political system. The policies of his party would go against him. They are not geared to give complete equality to all humans either in this "Western" society, or in poor, black, developing countries.

It is important to understand the need for authentic black leadership when moving towards black and white systems in partnership. Because we live in a black and white world, no race or system can be properly amalgamated before they are properly distinguished and plainly identified. Then a criterion of programmes, to be worked upon together and agreed, has to be drawn up in spite of the differences that now face the system. Apart from this simple, but unique evaluation, I doubt if society would ever safely ease the present unrest.

ARCHBISHOP-ELECT

From the IMCGB the Churches welcomed, voted for, supported and agreed upon, one of the most outstanding veterans of Pentecostalism to be elected in 1987 as the First Pentecostal Archbishop. The 1987 AGM of IMCGB, held on 18th July, came within the Convocation, from July 10th to 20th, of Shiloh United Church of Christ Apostolic worldwide (SUCCAW) which was attended by Churches' representatives from many parts of overseas countries and many parts of the UK. This AGM received the election of Bishop Malachi Ramsay, the Bishop of Shiloh United Church of Christ Apostolic Worldwide, to be the First Pentecostal Archbishop.

The joys expressed in the Convocation were almost uncontrollable. The shouts of "Glory Hallelujah!" and "Praise the Lord!" sent the sound meter leaping above maximum. In words of praise, people of all walks of life testified to the work done by the Bishop, now the Archbishop-elect, and most movingly from India and Africa.

The Indians produced training programmes given by the Archbishop-elect, translated into Indian languages, to be used for the teaching and development of the work of the Faith by Indian Ministers in India. The same praises and joy came from the Africans. So another work of God was done, as it is written in *Hebrews** 10, verse 7: "Then I said, 'Here I am – it is written about me in the scroll – I have come to do your will, O God.'" Thus the will of God was to be done.

THE WILL OF GOD

The call to do the will of God had come to black slaves, and now to their descendents. On my side, I was born in Jamaica in 1934, descended from an African great-grandmother and a white great-grandfather. This great-grandmother was a slave girl who was freed and worked as a nurse with my great-grandfather who was neither a slave nor a slave owner, but a doctor descended from a very distinguished Scottish family. His son and her daughter married. They were my father's parents. A revival originated in Jamaica in 1860-61, when what was to become the dominant strand of Christianity in Jamaica was born. Pentecostalism is the strongest strand of Christianity in Jamaica, the Caribbean and black America, and is becoming the dominant faith in most parts of Africa, and the fastest-growing, *Acts-of-the-Apostles** Christian faith throughout Britain today.

Our coming to Britain in the 50s was another part of the will of God begun. History began to write a new page when the new faces of black people arrived on the shores of Britain, south of which they once sailed in chains, under heavy guard, working, sweating, beaten, dying for the enrichment of their masters. They had worked also for their freedom. Being free, they came here, to be once more in bondage. Thus in the fourth generation from slavery, I was one among other members of that exodus who came here to face many experiences of hardships. Perhaps it was as hard for the Israelites under bondage in Egypt as it was for my

*The Holy Bible (NIV)

great-grandparents. It was even hard for us, the fourth generation of the victims of slavery, who have met the rejection, discrimination and unfair treatment experienced from the 50s to the 80s by us in Britain, which was to be home for most of us. But that is not my main subject.

The subject is Pentecostalism and the will of God: the mysteries of how God writes history among his people. His people must be delivered and they must deliver others, in the midst of the events of their slavery and in the midst of the journey of deliverance. For here, in Britain, out of the non-acceptance in the 50s, Pentecostalism began and by now has become a great ship in the desert. In the Christian life and in the life of the inner cities, the Church is a refuge among the many problems facing people of all ages, but mostly young people and young blacks who have lost their way, rescued through the faith of Pentecostal teaching. People of all races have gone off the course of Christian teaching.

Pentecostalism has that powerful force of bringing people back into line with the growing Church today, black and white preaching, teaching and learning together. The black and white men and women share the same status without reservation. Their status is the life in which they lead, serve and care for people. The people are moved by the work of the Office which they represent in the church, and how they are able to represent the Church organisation with openness to receive others who may not be identical in Christian tradition. The will of God has brought us this far, and the will of God has further written into the development of the Pentecostal faith an Archbishop. Thus God prepares the Church to work in the world to help save people from themselves and from the sin of others.

THE INAUGURATION OF
THE FIRST PENTECOSTAL ARCHBISHOP

The Archbishop's role must be a centre of focus for responsible, accountable and direct authenticity of one of the most visible hopes of partnership in faith and practice, bringing people together to meet their needs, save their souls from themselves and their enemies, for peace and justice and the keeping of law and order, equal opportunities, economic stability and good race relations. Since the spiritual liberation brought by John the Baptist, Jesus and the Apostles, coming to its climax on the Day of Pentecost around AD 33 at Jerusalem, the promise was to us and to as many as God shall call*.

The Archbishop was inaugurated on 9th July 1988. The Inauguration of Malachi Ramsay as Archbishop took place in his own Church, Shiloh United Church of Christ Apostolic Worldwide, at Lawrence Road in Croydon, London. It was a very colourful and joyful occasion.

Scriptures were read by Mrs. Janet Nightingale representing Christian Aid, Father Abiola of the Council of African and Afro-Caribbean Churches,

*See *The Acts of the Apostles* 2:39 in *The Holy Bible*.

Rev. Roswith Gerloff of the Ecumenical Center Christuskirche, Frankfurt/Main and our historian, Mrs. Rosalind Goodfellow and Rev. Hugh Cross representing the British Council of Churches, Rev. W. M. Wainwright of the Methodist Church, Senior Apostle J. O. Adegoke of the Centre for Black and White Christian Partnership and Rt. Rev. H. M. Vermeulen of Shiloh United Church of Christ Apostolic. Prayers were said by Rev. Colin Davey of the British Council of Churches, Rev. S. M. Douglas, General Secretary of IMCGB and Bishop Owusu-Akuffo of the Divine Prayer Society.

Rev. S. M. Douglas welcomed the many honoured guests representing many denominations, Councils and communities of the Christian Church from Britain and overseas. She read letters of greeting and prayerful good wishes from some of those unable to attend. Among these were the Prime Minister Mrs. Margaret Thatcher, Archbishop Robert Runcie, Archbishop of Canterbury, Archbishop John Habgood, Archbishop of York, Rt. Rev. Dr. Wilfred Wood, the Anglican Bishop of Croydon, Rt. Rev. Tony Dumper, Bishop of Dudley, and Mrs. Peggy Welch of the Catholic Association for Racial Justice.

His Grace the Archbishop of Canterbury wrote, "It was kind of you to invite me to the Inauguration of the First Pentecostal Archbishop at Shiloh Church of Christ Apostolic. Unfortunately I will not be able to attend personally, but I know there will be a representative from the British Council of Churches of which I am President. I take this opportunity of sending my greetings to the International Ministerial Council on the occasion of the Inauguration of Archbishop-elect Malachi Ramsay."

I, as Moderator, conducted the Inauguration ceremony and the Rev. V. Watson, Methodist Superintendent and Councillor of IMCGB officiated along with me at the Communion Service.

In his sermon the new Archbishop recalled the twenty years of planning and working that had led to this day, and said that "in the last six years we have got closer to the realisation of one of the philosophies which the Council has led us to see; that is, the necessity and possibility of the Unity of the Faith of all the people of God co-operating and serving in faith and spirit as the one Body of Christ".

Of himself, he said, "At the age of twenty years I answered God's call, and I vowed to follow

where He leads. In this, my fortieth year of service I recognise that there are no smooth paths, but His grace has never lost its strength. Today, I feel like Caleb*, who was one of the twelve who went to spy out the land of Canaan. He was forty years old when he accomplished that job and took back a good report. He did not deny that there were giants in the land, but confessed that the Israelites were well able to possess it."

Of the Church he said, "The Inauguration of the First Pentecostal Archbishop means that the Churches mean business, that they have work to do and they intend to do it with skill and determination."

The music for the Inauguration service was led by Brother Neville Burke and the Messiah's Heralds with joyful musicianship.

*See *Numbers 13:1-16* in *The Holy Bible*.

CHAPTER SEVEN

A Look at Pentecostalism

' *"I will make a new covenant....." declares the Lord. "I will put my law in their minds and write it on their hearts. I will be their God and they will be my people." '*

The Holy Bible (NIV), Jeremiah 31:31-33

BELIEFS AND STANDARDS
WHY JESUS CAME
THE TRUE VISION OF UNITY
WE CAN'T AFFORD TO FAIL THIS TIME

LAW AND ORDER AND THE CHURCH
SUMMING UP THE PENTECOSTAL FAITH
THE PHILOSOPHY OF PENTECOSTALISM
THE FIRST PENTECOSTAL ARCHBISHOP AND THE FUTURE

BELIEFS AND STANDARDS

While there are variations within Pentecostal Churches, there is a basic framework of beliefs and standards, liturgy and practice which one can expect to find in Pentecostalism. To explore the variety and history, I recommend *A Plea for British Black Theologies* by Roswith Gerloff published by Peter Lang.

Here is a concise summary of Christian teaching based on an essay by a thirteen year old girl brought up in the Trinitarian tradition. It also contains a brief description of worship and training in the Pentecostal tradition. Young people in Pentecostal Churches participate fully in worship, often taking a leading role in Church music and singing which are vitally important aspects of Pentecostal worship. They engage in serious studies of the Christian Faith of the New Testament.

"My Assembly worships in a hall which we hire, but some assemblies have their own Churches. Every day we worship God on our own, but on Sunday morning and evening, Monday Prayer Meeting, Wednesday Prayer Meeting and Bible Study, Thursday Choir Practice where we worship God with our voices in songs, and Friday Young Peoples' Meeting where we have Bible Studies and discussions, at all these times we come together to worship. On Saturdays there is usually a Convention at another Church or a concert. In the Church Service we worship by teaching, preaching, exulting, testifying, singing, clapping, reading the Scriptures and praying.

"The Bible is the Word from God. All things in it are inspired by God.
"God is three persons in one Godhead, the triune God, the Trinity. He is the Author and Creator of all things. His essence is love.
"The Father is the first person of the Trinity. He has planned our salvation. He sent Jesus to die for us, and the Holy Spirit to give us new life and power.
"Jesus is the Son of God, the second person of the Trinity. He died to forgive our sins and to give us true life.
"The Holy Spirit is the third person of the Trinity. A gift from God to us, he has the same power and should be obeyed.

"Baptism by the Holy Spirit takes place when we are filled with the Holy Spirit and speak in unknown tongues. He is given to us because we are saved.

"Man was created by God, originally created to praise God. Each man and woman is born and shaped through sin because of the Fall (The disobedience of the first man and woman).

"Sin is disobedience to God. The original sin was in the Garden of Eden and because of this we all inherit a sinful nature.

"Salvation is our rescue from being servants to sin to being servants to righteousness. "It takes place when we repent of our sins and accept the forgiveness made available by the death of Jesus.

"Angels are obedient servants of God and heirs of His Kingdom. They have a spiritual body.

"Demons are spirits who help Satan with his evil work.

"The Second Coming of Christ will take place when Jesus returns in person and believing people who are still living will be caught up in the skies to meet Him.

"The Church is the people of God who have received salvation through Christ and work together to worship and do His will.

"Divine healing is granted by God to us through the power of Christ who is able to do all things.

"Miracles are signs from God which show sinners that He truly is a miracle-working God and that His word is true. These signs awaken and establish faith in Jesus Christ. A miracle may, or may not, be contrary to normal expectations.

"The Lord's Supper (Holy Communion) is celebrated to acknowledge Christ's death by recalling in word and action His last supper with His disciples before He died.

"Feet-washing is when we follow the example of Christ who washed His disciples' feet. He taught them to serve one another, as He had come to serve and give His life for all people.

"Water Baptism is when a person is immersed in water. It takes place after conversion (when you turn to Christ in repentance) and is a sign of inner cleansing from sin, of death to our old life of disobedience, and of rising to a new life in Christ. We do not believe in sprinkling with water, but in immersion, which better represents our death to the old life of sin and resurrection to a new life in Christ, and it also represents the death, burial and resurrection of Jesus which makes our new life possible.

"A Convention is when we all come together from many Churches over a wide area to worship God together in spirit and in truth, and those people may be filled with the Holy Spirit. They are glad to see and encourage each other.
"Prayer is a way to commune with God and for Him to commune with us. It has many modes: adoration, thanksgiving, confession, supplication, intercession, spiritual warfare.
"Fasting is when we do without food and drink for a time as a spiritual exercise, following the example of Jesus.
"Hymns are songs of praise and worship which tell what God has done for us and of how we have experienced His goodness and mercy."

Pentecostals agree that full practice of New Testament teachings must be followed without fail, and Pentecostalism has to be Pentecostalism as set out in the Acts of the Apostles, with all the signs following: healing of the sick, looking after the poor, the saving of souls and the daily caring for other people to win them to be converted, by being sorrowful where the laws of God have been broken and bringing about changes so that they will not break them again. Then they seek baptism of water and baptism of the Spirit. Then they will receive the kind of gift about who or what you will be in the Church: cook, teacher, deacon, pastor, evangelist, cleaner, doorman, workman, lay member, healing vessel, Minister, Bishop, Social Worker etc. When these gifts are proven, the person's mission is stated and the Church will confirm his/her calling.

Many of the smaller types of Pentecostal Churches in Britain and elsewhere have not reached a stage of sophisticated organisation yet. They need time to bring themselves to the standard of Pentecostalism to be found in the two large streams of the foundation Churches: the Jesus Only and the Trinitarians. These small to-be-developed churches are mainly African or Asian orientated and I have discovered from discussions that a highly critical view is held, by politicians and denominational clergy, of them as being merely sects among new religions in Europe. The same was said about Pentecostals, now established, when we started here in the 50s. Now we are the most admired Churches among the British Churches in our worship, life-style and down-to-earth doctrinal interpretations and evangelism.

The so-called "new religions" were discussed in the BCC, by individual Churches by other Church Councils and Euro-MPs. How those practising in this country and elsewhere will be affected depends largely on their adherence to standards of moral living, spiritual practice, best practice in management and pastoral ethics, property and financial matters, as well as how they set about recruiting membership and who they allow to be recognised as licensed practitioners in the Ministry, and to bear titles of high office. These issues must be carefully studied.

The IMCGB has a standard guideline agreed upon as to methods and practice within the Pentecostal faith. It is expected that these guidelines will be followed by all Pentecostal Churches, both members of IMCGB and non-members. The terms of reference include the selection and ordination of all Church Officers and the Code of Conduct they must follow. These accord with the New Testament practice of Jesus Christ and the Apostles, and they have been submitted to the Home Office as part of the practising philosophy and organisational structure of the IMCGB.

WHY JESUS CAME

Jesus Christ came into the world to fulfil the law *(Matthew 5:26). He gave himself for us by His death and resurrection, and by our belief, repentance, baptism by water and by the Holy Spirit and by holy living daily in the pattern of the life of Jesus and the Apostles, the law is written in our hearts. "I will put my laws in their minds and write them in their hearts." (Hebrews 8:10) We have gone beyond the letter of the Law of the Old Testament to the underlying principles as in *Romans**, chapter 14 verse 17, "For the Kingdom of God is not a matter of eating and drinking, but of righteousness, peace and joy in the Holy Spirit." Pentecostals look at reasons for the coming of Jesus Christ into the world from prophecies in the Old Testament and the giving of His life

*See *The Holy Bible, Exodus* chapter 20. **See *The Holy Bible (NIV)*

in exchange for ours. This becomes effective when we believe in Him. He had died to save us from complete loss. The story started in *Genesis* *, chapter 1, when the soul of man was put in a body and made to live, and eventually to live on as God's ever-living accomplishment. It went wrong and went on and on and on throughout the Old Testament and just could not become right even with all the help and chastisement given. Jesus came to put that right through a well designed, but simple way, that if we can accept that He is the Lord and Saviour of the world and that He can save us, if we follow His command of repentance, baptism and receiving the Holy Spirit, and abide in the new testament of His death through obedience and keep the teaching of the New Testament Gospel without any of the made-up diversions going about these days, then there is hope for us to live after death. There is hope that we will be raised a sinless person and become again a body as described in *Genesis* in the story of Adam and Eve before they sinned and received a dying body. Jesus is the Way, the Truth and the Life**. No one will come to the Father except through Him. Not by keeping the Law. Not by keeping the Ten Commandments. At our own free will we must take up our cross and go after Him, meaning living the way He lived and taught us to live and serving Him in obedience.

The Law of the Old Testament, because of the inability of people to reach its standards, could not save even those people to whom it was given as a special sign of God's love and determination to identify them as His people. The New Testament saves everybody who will follow the teaching and is prepared to give up the other, less everlasting short and sweet thought that when you are dead you are finished.

Some Pentecostals prove positive in the hope of achieving the repeating of the Day of Pentecost for the complete unification of the various traditions in Christian worship, to come to one vast, quick, united force to convert those who must receive the Gospel of Jesus Christ before the return of the Son of Man to claim the everlasting Church of the Kingdom of God on earth.

*See *The Holy Bible*, **See *The Holy Bible, John* 14:6

THE TRUE VISION OF UNITY

This salvation was not confined to one race of people or one religion, as the old salvation was to Judaism, but it was for whoever was willing to receive it. *Luke**, chapter 12, verse 8 reads, "Whoever acknowledges me before men, the Son of Man will also acknowledge him before the angels of God." *Matthew**, chapter 12, verse 50 says, "Whoever does the will of my Father in heaven is my brother and sister and mother." 1 *John**, chapter 5, verse 1 reads, "Everyone who believes that Jesus is the Christ is born of God."

For the first time both Jews and Gentiles were free to receive salvation, and men had seen God in the flesh. For the first time, men were given a new way to be born again and to live again. Man had his first chance to be free by a choice of his own conviction, to choose life for once, a chance to live again as Christ lived again, as Lazarus** lived again.

When we are baptised, when we take up the Cross, that is when we start to live and work as that kind of person, then we know we are becoming a Pentecostal. That unique change does not make us into a different person physically, but new in mind and thought and daily living. We could still keep our old job if it was morally honest. We could still be going to our old Church. We could keep some, if not all, of our old friends. It is just that the change in us will be seen by others who may not understand, but we know we are new in spirit and thoughts and attitudes. As to how clear to others it is, it is them, and not us, who know. Some will condemn. Some will praise. They did the same to Jesus. The wonderful change brought by this new testament is that every single Christian tradition and form of organisation and individual person could take this new testament that Jesus brought, and be transformed. They would worship as Pentecostals, teach as Pentecostals, care as Pentecostals, praise God as Pentecostals, suffer together as Pentecostals, live as Pentecostals, rejoice as Pentecostals and receive blessings and spiritual enrichment together as Pentecostals. There is no need for us to change our names in order to work together in this way: Roman Catholic, Anglican, Orthodox, Congregational, United Free, United Reformed, Lutheran, Methodist, Baptist, Bethel Apostolic, Shiloh Apostolic, Calvary Church of God in Christ, New

*See *The Holy Bible (NIV)*, **See *The Holy Bible, Luke* 24;34 and *John* 11:38-44

Testament Church of God in Christ, …..CTBI, IMCGB, WCC, WRRO, AWUCOC, Allied Council of African Churches….we can all have this united way of working in a spiritual and united mind, pooling resources, working much closer to balance the strain of separation brought since man was first made responsible. This was the unique change Christ brought in the new testament. The drama acted out by Christ on the night He was betrayed reflects the difficulty of such a unique plan to remove all barriers to our working together in His Kingdom. We will be betrayed constantly until we all come to the unity of the faith and to the knowledge of the truth in Christ. The drama of that night is before us in the world. As far as Jesus Christ is concerned, all the labels and names in the world do not impress Him. He is interested in our being born again into Pentecostalism which He brought to us so that we might inherit the Kingdom.

How clear and simple is the one truth: that there is no hope in any other salvation than the Salvation to which Jesus Christ called men, women and children, calling them to follow the way He lived and worked. He fed, healed, counselled, taught, helped, rebuked, cast out devils, prayed, preached, fasted, raised the dead. He was mobbed, beaten, angered, hungered, tempted, persecuted, stripped of clothes, chased, arrested, mocked, charged and was killed. Sad and horrible for us to think about and for Jesus to experience for us to see His love, and how serious He is about us coming with Him. He called men that time too, and let them take over when He had showed them what to do and had empowered them by His Spirit. Some of those people met the same fate as He did, some met worse, but they came together and did as they were told. We have the book of *The Acts of the Apostles** which tells us what happened to the people Jesus left behind and how they continued the work Jesus gave them to do. We have other books of the *New Testament** written by these Apostles, that give closer and more personalised accounts of their work, their lives, their thinking and experiences. That account was the full, the one and final foundation before the return of Jesus Christ. He will be coming for a people who live, work, think, care together and are prepared to protect each other, for the love of, and in obedience to, Him.

*See *The Holy Bible*

WE CAN'T AFFORD TO FAIL THIS TIME

Man's life was badly affected from the Fall of man. God confessed that the enemy would bruise His heel, but He would bruise the enemy's head*.

Pentecostalism is the only way ahead for the world to become the sort of place any sound-thinking person will want to see, and it is the only power that is able to change the nations of the world. The ultimate decisions must be the Church's.

We must, in a short time, come to an understanding of what the Church is about and come to work together. My fear is that constant self-will may bring this result: that God will decide that we have failed again, and may cause Churches who resist the true call and practice of Pentecostalism to be diminished.

(I do not refer to the churches labelled "Pentecostal". God is not impressed by labels. I mean by "Pentecostalism" those who enter the Kingdom of Heaven.)

We see some evidence of this over the past ten to fifteen years. Churches are being sold to private developers and the people have vanished. Many excuses have been made. Some of those Church buildings have been bought by poor, black congregations of Pentecostal Churches. Pentecostalism does not decrease, it increases. Since Jesus called the first disciples, the Kingdom of Heaven has been increasing, and since John the Baptist preached, calling for men to prepare for it, men and women have continued to flow into it. In spite of killings and the risks involved, the numbers have continued to grow. They must grow rapidly as people accept the free and full Salvation set up by God through Jesus Christ. It is only by means of this objective that man will ever reach his maximum opportunity to know his real value. The cost to achieve this maximum goal of life, and freedom for ever, is that we were bought with a price beyond measure.

We also are to take up our cross**. The perception many have of Pentecostal worship as being noisy and "happy-clappy" is mistakenly naïve. Pentecostals practise a serious asceticism, as strict and

*See *The Holy Bible, Genesis* 3:15, **See *The Holy Bible, Mark* 8: 34

demanding as any monastic order, but carried out amid the stress of inner-city working and family life. It is a life of self-sacrifice and discipline so that each may serve God according to his/her calling. It involves serving communities and suffering various kinds of insult and persecution for Christ's sake. The public worship may or may not be noisy, but it is part of Pentecostal asceticism as the worshippers, by praise and adoration, enter the presence of God and are caught up in adoration, seeking Holy Spirit anointing. They seek Holy Spirit anointing, Holy Spirit gifts, the grace to practise holy living, deliverance, and empowerment to reach new levels of service and new dimensions of Ministry also, by the disciplines of prayer and fasting at different levels and through spiritual warfare and knowledge of and obedience to the Bible as the Word of God. They do this in order that the Church as a whole may be built up to carry out the ministry in the world that Christ called her to: baptising, healing, casting out demons, preaching and teaching the Kingdom of heaven. Both lay people and clergy take part in these disciplines. Most Pentecostals abstain from alcohol and cigarette smoking.

LAW AND ORDER AND THE CHURCH

Jesus said, "My Kingdom is not of this world."* How then does the Church relate to the communities in which it operates? Take the United Kingdom, for example.

The breakdown of discipline in schools in the UK, the serious rise in crime in the community and the breakdown of law and order are very grave misfortunes that cannot be divorced from one another, as feeding pipelines, working in conjunction with one another to produce devastating effects on the rest of the community. Some of the saddest experiences developed must have largely begun with the breakdown of discipline in the classroom and looseness at home. Some of those bad experiences are set out in the Report on the Brixton Disorders, 10-12 April 1981**, by Lord Scarman, OBE. There were other serious inner city riots and disorders, other than Brixton. There was Liverpool and Birmingham and Manchester and other places, and, of course, the Printers' Strikes and the Miners' Strikes. It would seem unlikely that the girl who, at the age of 13 wrote that account*** of her faith and the Church she had been attending since she was eight weeks old, would be mixed up in any sort of street crime or serious disorder. There has been a decline in faith. Churches cannot wash their hands of failure. Many government departments, local and national, have failed to address the real issues. Elements in the media and education have encouraged life-style tendencies that create aggression.

We all have to take our share of the blame. As long as we represent, or claim to represent, any section of society and make decisions that will affect the lives of others, we must carry some kind of blame or we would be charged as irresponsible. People reflect only what is imposed upon them by the system which governs each area of their lives. These systems are decided upon by other people: employers at work; the bank for money; the Post Office for mail; stores and markets for food, clothes and materials; industries for products; parents for children; government for law, order, transport, health etc.; schools for education; local government for local affairs; and the Church for faith, morality,

*See *The Holy Bible, John* 18:36. **Report of an enquiry into the Brixton Disorders 10-12 April 1981, available from Her Majesty's Stationery Office.
***See pages 114 – 115 above. .

lifestyle, and challenge to government. All these institutions are run by people. They are processed by a system riddled with principalities and powers outside the borders of the Kingdom of God. The Church is a vital part of this system and may be seen sometimes to work with the system in unrighteousness, while remaining as if it were innocent, clean and powerless.

No one is saying the Church is to oppose the system all the time, but it cannot take part in that which has imperilled humanity by sinful behaviour. Discrimination is in the Church on a large scale*. Whilst it may claim to make no conditions as to who may come to Church and who may become members with regard to sex and colour, look at the staff and clergy! The black people in these Churches are not without blame, because some of them think they are not their brother's keeper,** and going to a white-led Church is a step up in class. What matters is the imbalance it places on the faith, the deprivation it brings to the weak, the waste of strengthening the strong, making richer those who are rich, comforting the comforted. Where is the reasoning power to strike a balanced argument for a possibility of parity in a system designed to make certain people eat the crumbs that fall from the tables of other?***

It is not enough to make a few black people Stewards, Lay Preachers and Ministers. There needs to be a balance of equality in leadership in proportion to the membership, and there should be examples of black Ministers in charge of white congregations.

Furthermore the Church cannot sit comfortably in the bosom of an atheist government. In the presence of Jesus every knee shall bow and every tongue acknowledge Him. The Church must not and cannot interfere with what is right and just, but it is the Church's duty to tell the highest and mightiest powers of the world to make amends for wrongs. If the Government is a Christian Government, (and the world believes that Britain is a Christian country) Church and State should be

---

*These words were written in 1992. Since then the indigenous Churches have addressed this issue, largely as a result of the work of IMCGB in presenting this challenge through the ecumenical bodies, Churches Together in Britain and Ireland (CTBI) and Churches Together in England (CTE). It is a problem which does not disappear overnight, but needs constant research and vigilance.
**See *The Holy Bible*, Genesis 4:8-12, ***See *The Holy Bible*, Luke 16:19-21.

working together as partners, sharing responsibilities in the fields of service where there is common ground. Every good government should want to work with the Church and there should be no hesitation by the Church in accepting this role as long as the Church remembers that its terms of reference must be justice for all, as all are created by God. If the Churches are in full unity, then the Government will have to give serious attention to the Churches, because Churches are made up of people and governments are elected by people.

Present attitudes raise four questions. 1) Does the Church really care about the present injustices? 2) Do the Church Leaders really understand what Christianity means? 3) Do Churches truly want partnership in working, sharing and living together? 4) Do they accept *The Acts of the Apostles*, and do they accept that the Churches will not manage to live and work and share together unless there is an outpouring of the Spirit, as in The *Acts of the Apostles* chapter 2? England has a problem similar to the one experienced by the people in *The Acts*. It can only be dealt with by the Pentecostal Fire* that must fall in the UK. It must also fall elsewhere, because there have never been any other plans to bring the people of the world to a clear life of certainty of peace and justice, before the return of Jesus to take His place as Head of every nation.

Peace in the world can come only when men have all things in common. *The Acts of the Apostles,* chapter 2, verses 41-47 says that they had all things in common, because they all had the same thinking in mind as to what they had to do.The Church stands as the Author of peace on earth for all men, and asks for justice.The Church must learn that failure to speak on the issues can prevent justice, not only for the poor, the blacks, the gays, women, the youth, handicapped, old and infirm, but also for the high and mighty. The government and the Church must be seen to be doing justice together.

*See *The Holy Bible, Acts* 2:1-4

SUMMING UP THE PENTECOSTAL FAITH

Jesus Christ brought Pentecostalism to change the world, and intended a total reformation. We are told it was God's idea in real terms of liberation from sin, idolatry and slavery, to freedom and justice for all.

It began in the Old Testament with Moses commissioned by God to free the Children of Israel. They are the symbol of a free nation, delivered from Egypt, which is the symbol of a nation in slavery, representing both the oppressor and the oppressed: an idea of the good that has run into constant obstructions preventing the complete success of God's plans. Each shows the damaging effects caused by the enemy. From Moses to Jesus Christ things always went wrong. If you like, they went wrong from the time of Adam. The Moses' commission was to recover mistakes on a larger scale, at a more supervised level with more restrictive controls. These measures have never worked, except for a few.

Jesus then introduced a system that has all power not to fail again, and one that is irreversible and will destroy the enemy finally. That was not what the Father, the Son and the Holy Spirit wanted. They had hoped that the enemy would become a friend, for, sadly, the enemy are people created by God. God hopes that they may change to good by His simpler appeal through Jesus Christ. Pentecostals believe that Christ came and introduced the system of the restitution, allowing himself to be killed and raised from the dead to show that He is indestructible. He gave an extension of time to the enemies to change through the hearing of the message of redemption and to make up their mind freely. God will not force anyone to accept what He gave to everyone for the taking.

When that extension of time is ended, then the Kingdom of God will take control of the purifying of the world and separating the enemies from the friends of God. All the enemies of God and their works will be banished, says the Word of God through Jesus Christ and the prophets, Apostles, Ministers and servants of the Faith.

Pentecostalism means no more and no less than what is recorded in the four *Gospels** of the *New Testament*, the work done in *the Acts of the Apostles**, the *Epistles** of the *New Testament* and the final account of the prophecy of *The Revelation**, as to what will take place at that time of the final restitution. In the same manner as Moses and the prophets in the *Old Testament** worked on the Laws and the prophecies and told of the coming of Christ and His life, death and resurrection, mostly by *Daniel**, *Ezekiel**, *Jeremiah** and, clearest of all, *Isaiah**. John, in *The Revelation**, prophesied the coming of Christ back into the world for the restitution of all things. "Therefore keep watch, because you do not know on what day your Lord will come."**

THE PHILOSOPHY OF PENTECOSTALISM

Pentecostalism is to bring friends very close together in works and belief, caring and sharing, and, above all, loyalty to each other and a code of clear identification which distance or issues cannot conceal.

According to Pentecostalism we are to love one another as Christ loved us.*** This is to love any friend of God. Then Jesus said, we are to love and feed our enemies also.**** There are a number of reasons why we should love and feed an enemy, although with caution. Friends most times are not in need, because they often have access to our resources and can sometimes help themselves if they just tell us, whilst our enemies may be in need and we fail to notice. Secondly, we stand a chance of turning an enemy into a friend, by using the understanding of caring for him or her. Pentecostalism is based on this. The black Pentecostal Churches in UK, USA and the West Indies are based on this. It is upon *The Acts of the Apostles** and Jesus Christ that these black-led Churches are set up and run. That is, the genuine Churches. There are con-men here, there and everywhere, and some even imitate Churches, but have another agenda. Some think there is money in Pentecostalism, and power and fame as well, if they are not found out. There have been con-men from the days of the Apostles. Jesus said,

*See *The Holy Bible,* **See *The Holy Bible (NIV), Matthew* 24:42,
***See *The Holy Bible, John* 15:12-14. ****See *The Holy Bible, Matthew* 5:43-48.

"Watch out for false prophets." Some tried to buy power from Peter for money*. Some people have even been converted while listening to the Bible being read by one of these con-men! The words they were reading were God's words, which have power to change those who believe. At the same time, the so-called leader who is a fraud will find himself judged by the Word of God.

I believe Pentecostalism to be the only way of changing this world, of solving the various problems of man, personal, social, political, military and strategic, bringing total peace and equality for all. Then there will be the complete cessation of man's worst enemies: death, destruction, incurable diseases. First, serious attempts must be made between all faiths and religions, political and social groupings and the Christian Churches to observe the coming of Jesus Christ into the world, with Pentecostalism as the final remedy to cure mankind and secure all people as beneficiaries of the Kingdom. Pentecostalism is created as the ship to safety. The Christian Churches are really sitting on top of an ocean of responsibility, because they are the ones who claim that they have it right. Since they have it right, they have to do the works of righteousness to reveal righteousness. The Christian Churches today must not allow their apparent righteousness to be self-righteousness, which would look very much the same as in the time of Moses and the prophets. Hardly anyone was willing to do what had to be done. In the time of Jesus, they persecuted, imprisoned and killed those who were willing to do what needed to be done. In this society they sit back and let you work to a state of self-destruction and suffering, wounded by their negative attitudes and selfishness, controlled by the imperial laws of man-made old Roman justice. To that kind of justice Jesus gave its true perspective when he said, "Give to Caesar what is Caesar's, and to God what is God's."** Both the Government and the Church must be called in question to declare who is who and what is what. What will be the role of government in the saving of souls, for the restoration of peace and justice for all and the true implementation of law and order, arising from respect for God, then for one another? What will be the role of the Church in relation to Government, and by what method will the Government govern a Christian country whose Queen is Head of

---

*See *The Holy Bible*, Acts 8:18-24. **See *The Holy Bible (NIV)*, Matthew 22:21.

State and Church, to prevent power, given by the election of a minority, (by a majority voting system), being used for the benefit of individuals who seek to use power, not as it was intended as a trust given, but as a platform of gimmickry and the exploitation of the underprivileged poor people of a Christian country? How prevent the creation of a class of rich and powerful "dives" of this world, at whose table the poor eat the crumbs that fall? The people do not know what they look like in real life, but they know them on TV as immortals. The Church and the State must soon get much closer together to restructure both sides to provide a more reformed type of people-to-people Church-and-Government care-structure in place of the distance-apart ones now in existence. This would certainly fit in with the message of the Kingdom of God to come, in which we believe.

The mind of the King of kings, thinking of and caring for the entirety of heaven and earth, must be incomprehensible to our small understanding. It is such simple, down-to-the-manger type King-mind at work, solving what the high and mighty could not be bothered with. It is the great mystery, to create nothing into something. The ultimate goal is to save those who want to be saved, because they do not see themselves as too high and mighty to be saved by the one, universal King of kings and His simple, mysterious, caring methods. This is the mind of God and His Son Jesus Christ, who are to come here soon to complete the implementation of this fantastic piece of spiritual legislation for the well-being of those who devoted their life and service for it. It shall go on and on and on. There will be no complaints, for we will all have shared responsibility and full participation.

This is one of the reasons my colleagues and myself in some of the various Churches, some black, some white, feel we have to work so hard and do the many different things we do, to bring home to others the message. We have done our work the best way that conditions and needs, placed before us by the Holy Spirit, allowed. We did not ask questions of how or where we should get money, or property, or food. The Lord Jesus Christ and His Apostles suffered many things. The apostles too had no access to large bank balances and profits and properties, but we read that they pooled their resources together and they went about spreading the Gospel daily and they had all things in common.

THE FIRST PENTECOSTAL ARCHBISHOP AND THE FUTURE

In electing a Pentecostal Archbishop we mean to demonstrate that God is no respecter of persons in terms of colour, politics, race, religion, sex, class or need. He respects us on terms of our service, having called us to serve one another in various ranks, but by the same Spirit. We need an Archbishop for accountability and reference of identification in the UK and the world at large. Those who feel that this is wrong will have some long and documented talking to do, to justify their view from both theological and doctrinal points. We would, on the evidence in hand, show such people are living out of times and out of touch with Europe and the rest of the Christian world. The system of an archbishop has very little to do with one's soul as a Christian, or even one's belief, but the office is designated to bring unity and make exchange of Faith and experience a much more rock-bottom practice. It is to secure certain formalities for the freedom and trust necessary to facilitate and stimulate a working relationship between Heads of States and Heads of Churches for the development and supportive sharing with one another of the various resources for the spreading of the Gospel throughout the world, so that we may act as a united force to meet the shortfall of human morality and dignity, to solve together the discord of the ages, that now spells "once upon a time".

A momentous experience of fulfilment for the black-led Churches came on 12th and 13th July 1991, when Roswith Gerloff's thorough research and writing and working amongst us was recognised and rewarded as she received her doctorate from Birmingham University. On 13th July a celebration was held for Dr. Roswith Gerloff at Calvary Church of God in Christ, Luton, when the two volumes of her thesis, *A Plea for British Black Theologies**, were on display. There was great rejoicing and some of the younger men and women began to realise, for the first time, the long, hard road that we had already trodden and the size of the victories won.

These great events received no media coverage although they were historic moments in the life of the black-led Churches and of the whole Church. By its omissions the media would seem to distort the facts of

---

*Published by Peter Lang.

life in this country and would seem to portray by silence and absence that religion, and in particular, caring Christianity, is dead.

Similarly, another great occasion, the Inauguration of the Council of Churches for Britain and Ireland (CCBI)*, was not considered newsworthy, although TV cameras were present. This was a great landmark in British Church history. Large and small Churches, Councils and Church organisations had been working to set up a new ecumenical instrument to replace the British Council of Churches. At last, in 1990 all our work came to fruition. On 8th September the Churches in the British Isles came together in one body, the Council of Churches for Britain and Ireland, at a spectacular ceremony in Liverpool. That was the first time since the Great Schism of 1054 that Eastern Orthodox and Western Churches had joined together. It was the first time since the Reformation of the 16th century that the Roman Catholic Churches had joined with Reformed Churches. For the first time, also, black-led Churches are full members of the united body of Churches.

The ceremony was colourful. After the Service of Worship in Liverpool Cathedral, the clergy and representatives of all the Churches walked from that Cathedral to the Metropolitan Cathedral a mile away. Those at the beginning of the procession, turning to look back when they arrived at the Metropolitan Cathedral, saw the whole mile of road completely filled with people processing, some just leaving the Liverpool Cathedral. On the way, the Archbishops and other leaders were heckled by the Rev. Ian Paisley and his supporters who were unhappy about the healing of these centuries old separations. And all this was not newsworthy. The Churches, like the black people, remained invisible by omission. Yet they are people, like all other British Citizens. They are voters in a democracy, having equal status and rights with all other citizens. It is an intolerance and injustice to attempt to render us invisible.

*Now Churches Together in Britain and Ireland(CTBI).

We are pleased, however, that the Inauguration of Churches Together in England* (CTE), the English arm of CCBI, *was* shown on television.

We are happy also, that our work is welcomed and recognised by others who are discerning. The IMCGB is included in the 1989 edition of Canons B43 and B44 of the Ecumenical Measures of the Church of England. The Canons lay down the Code of Practice of the Church of England in relation to other Churches and Local Ecumenical Projects. It is the duty of the Archbishops of Canterbury and York to designate those Churches which may be included in the provisions of the Canons.**

We now look forward to the dawn of a new day, not laying a new foundation, because it was already there and Christ is the Chief Cornerstone***, followed by the Apostles and prophets and ourselves to complete the building into a spiritual house. On these principles we have a duty to carry out the work of God, not as novices, but as Ministers and servants of God together, not going over again the mistakes of the past, but looking towards working together as one nation of the household of faith in Christ.

*See the "Basis of Commitment" on page 157 ** See *Ecumenical Relations Canons B43 and B44: Code of Practice* on page 31, published by the General Synod of the Church of England. ***See *The Holy Bible, Ephesians* 2:19-22

CHAPTER EIGHT

No Longer Strangers, but Pilgrims Together

"You are no longer foreigners and aliens, but fellow-citizens with God's people and members of God's household, built on the foundation of the apostles and prophets, with Christ Jesus Himself as the Chief Cornerstone."

The Holy Bible (NIV), Ephesians 2:19-20

PENTECOSTALISM AND IMMIGRATION
THE CONTRIBUTION OF BLACK PEOPLE TO BRITAIN
EVIDENCES

PENTECOSTALISM AND IMMIGRATION

Pentecostalism is integral to the Body of Christ. It must be in every Church, if not now, then sooner or later. Where Christ is worshipped in Spirit and in truth, Pentecost must come. In an imperfect world, the Christian must live as normal and as simple a life as possible, obeying God. They cannot be brainwashed to do this or that, but must do things so they can see for themselves and learn from their own experiences through success or failure. If they fail they are to keep on trying, and God will help them, lead them and carry them through.

Pentecostalism, to us as black people, as mixed-race people, as multicultural people, is the true messenger of ecumenism.

Jesus commissioned His disciples to "Make disciples of all nations," and Peter, to whom after his confession to Jesus, "You are the Christ", Jesus had said, "On this rock I will build my Church**", affirmed, "The promise is for you and your children and for all who are far off, -- for all whom the Lord our God will call.***"*

Between 1948 and 1992 immigrants coming to the UK have amounted to more than one million, among that number being people of several faiths: Sikhism, Islam, Buddhism, Judaism, Jainism, Hinduism, Christianity and others. Among a large number of immigrants came Pentecostalism from the Caribbean and Africa, supported from the USA and Canada, linking with parts of Europe. The largest proportion of people applying to come to England in the name of Church Ministry or Church orientated mission were black and Pentecostal. The largest proportion of new people coming in to try to spread the Gospel are

*See *The Holy Bible (NIV)*, Matthew 28:19. **See *The Holy Bible (NIV)*, Matthew 16:16-18. ***See *The Holy Bible (NIV)*, The Acts of the Apostles, 2:39.

Pentecostally orientated. The fastest-growing body over the world today, through some form of migration is Pentecostalism.

Many young black and mixed race people and their parents understand that Pentecostalism is a force designed by Jesus Christ to spread the Gospel. The Apostles and Jesus Christ in the first place, whom we follow, were seen as travellers in the same terms. They were treated with fear, reservation, rejection, and were made strong by the sufferings and misfortunes that were to produce the challenge. All the challenges that we meet do not lessen our faith, our calling, our duty and our will to recognise our great blessing when, in the first instance, we were called to be removed from our country of origin by force as slaves, in the second instance we were privileged, some of us, to become part of more than one race of people, thirdly, a few of us, fortunately or unfortunately, came out of lines of distinction, fourthly, we were taught by those who enslaved us an ambiguous fragment of Christianity, which was to open our eyes to discover later the ambiguity of their sincerity, and fifthly we have the privilege, through the calling of God, to be able to live inside the heart of the land from whence those who enslaved us came, having sailed past in chains, to return there to stay as immigrants under the banners of subjects and citizens, carrying the banner of salvation, called Pentecostalism, working together with some of those who were once strangers and masters, and now are becoming, not strangers, but Pilgrims together in Christ*. This is what we are called to in the declaration of faith in the ecumenical instrument of the Council of Churches for Britain and Ireland and Churches Together in England.

---

*See the *Swanwick Declaration* in *Churches Together in Pilgrimage*, page 7, published by BCC.

Pentecostalism was founded amidst racism experienced between Jews, Gentiles and Samaritans, and then persecution and bloodshed along with other kinds or repression. The success of Christianity spreading from Jerusalem to the uttermost parts of the earth was due to the very people who were victims of the repression of justice and peace. They triumphed through the liberation that Jesus Christ brought when He founded the Pentecostal Church. True Pentecostal practice must be taught and practiced starting at "Jerusalem", to our children and their children and whoever God shall call, near or far. We learn from sadness, loss and grief, that strength and success must come, if not in our lifetime, then to our offspring.

In carrying out the will of Jesus Christ we stand in the line of succession of the apostles in the Kingdom of God. That succession is entered into, not, as some claim, by means of an unbroken chain of hands laid by one ordained Minister upon another to commission him to the Ministry, in an unbroken line traced back to St. Peter. God is omnipotent, omnipresent and invisible. He works through us by His Spirit, by His power and inspiration, by and through being born again by Christ's blood that was shed, by water and the Spirit. Pentecostal Ministers are very much like the apostles. They are chosen to be Ministers of one kind or another from being lay members of the Church, drawn from all parts of society and situations, factory engineers, sweepers, solicitors, teachers, office workers, railway porters, nurses, doctors, social workers, and so on. Ninety per cent of Ministers are not paid. They themselves have to contribute money towards the running of the Church. It may take years before a Minister will receive a small allowance for travel and expenses. After a long period of planning and investment he or she may be able to provide a small stipend for himself and some of the other Ministers. Pentecostal Churches have many Ministers, so that the workload is carried in a shared manner, so that a full day-to-day programme can be maintained by a fully staffed Ministry, without a salaried Minister. We carry with the Ministry a heavy social responsibility and most of our finance goes into that, into buildings, evangelism, immigration advice and community projects.

We encourage our Government to grant asylum to those who are forced to seek a place of refuge, recognising that history has turned back upon itself. There were explorations in the 16th century, colonisation and the slave trade in the 17th century, the Age of Reason in the 18th century, the exploration of Africa in the 19th century, and now people from those countries which Europeans "discovered" and took over in those periods have been coming to Europe. Because of this, there is more and more fascination with and serious study of a variety of religions, especially by young people in schools. Black people have brought, in Pentecostalism, the richness of a new experience in the Christian life in and through immigration.

THE CONTRIBUTION OF BLACK PEOPLE TO BRITAIN

After forty years of Pentecostalism in England, people still have not understood what all these new faces and changes are about.

People are asking three questions? Why did black people come to Britain in the first place? What have they contributed to this country? Are they going to return to where they came from?

My answer to the third question is that between 1948 and 1992 more than one third of the black people who came here have returned to their own country or moved on to other countries in Europe, USA, Canada, a few even to Australia. Perhaps half that number, retired or now reaching retirement age, will return to their country of origin. These belong to the first generation of immigrants. We are now looking at the second and third generations who have increased in number by at least four times that of the first generation. They will not be going back anywhere. This is their home. Where their great-grandparents and grandparents came from is now interesting history to them. It will be helpful to their education in school and college. Every effort should be made so that the younger generations can know it all in detail.

As for question one, black people were invited from Commonwealth countries in the late 1940s, after the second world war to help rebuild Britain, which was devastated and without much of its labour force. Post war chaos brought poverty, distress, hardships and sickness causing more deaths to add to the millions lost during the war. The Health Service needed personnel, so did transport, the building trade and manufacturing. Food from overseas needed to be handled by those who came from where it was produced, with knowledge and understanding. Farms, poultry and agriculture needed workers. The mines for coal and coke, the motor car and truck industries, London and County bus companies were all looking for staff. Britain needed to make money and compete in imports and exports if she was going to get back on her feet. The black people were asked to come and do the hard tasks, skilled, semi-skilled and labouring jobs. In every sphere black people sweated and laboured with what was left of their white brothers. That was why they were here.

In answer to question two, black people have worked beyond expectations in speed and strength and loyalty, sweating and struggling in the face of many abuses and much resentment, in all sections of industry and commerce, health, welfare, transport, building, imports, exports, whatever it took to rebuild Britain. Besides this, they have made considerable contributions in arts, crafts, music and sport. Above all, they have made an invaluable contribution to inter-Church, inter-religious ecumenical richness in variety, style and success. They have contributed to better community relations and have set a new hope for the future in law and order, equal rights and enrichment of cultural examples.

EVIDENCES

It is a mark of Pentecostalism that we see our own story as the continuation of the Old and New Testament stories. God's will is acted out in history. He gives life and takes life. We come into this world at birth unaware of ourselves, and when we die we become unaware that we are dead. Yet we were born and we do die. Jesus said, "I am the Resurrection and the life. He who believes in me will live, even though he dies*." I rejoice that, although the work recorded in this book was accomplished through pain and sorrow, yet there is a better life to come. Some people say we have no evidence that people live again.

*See *The Holy Bible (NIV), John* 11:25.

The books recording the life and teaching of Jesus have been subjected to enormous scrutiny because those who want to say, "There is no God" and "There is no life after death", have levelled what they hoped would be destructive criticisms at the books. However, each criticism has led to extensive and meticulous research, and this has established beyond doubt the reliability of these records. Some of the criticisms that have been put forward and answered* are: how trustworthy are the biographies of Jesus and can they stand up to scrutiny?; have they been preserved down the centuries in such a way that we can rely on them?; is there evidence for Jesus in any other ancient literature and does archaeological evidence confirm the biographies or contradict them?; is the historical Jesus the same as the Jesus worshipped by Christians? Christian scholars have written many books to help us access all the evidence we need.

Since there are all these evidences of life after death and of our accountability, it is folly for a person to disregard his Maker or think he is so great that he can ignore the fact that, in relation to God upon whom the prolonging or ending of life depend, he is a subject.

---

*The editor suggests a brief summary of findings and a list of scholarly works for further investigation can be found in *The Case for Christ* by Lee Strobel, Harper Collins, ISBN 0 310 20930 7, and *Bad, Mad or God?* By John Redford, St. Pauls Publishing, ISBN 085439 694 2.

All the sufferings we have been through, in pain and sadness, in love and faith, in the work of God, are endurable because of the greater joy of that new life in a new body to which we look forward. The history of my family and of Pentecostalism is a picture of this. This is the mystery of how we were taken from Africa as slaves, to the Caribbean, how we became part of a mixed-race family of high esteem, as well as coming from a black ancestral family of distinction, how we became free again as part of a Commonwealth, though with some disadvantages, how we came back to the heart of the country of those who once claimed to be our masters, *now our partners, how we have worked to become witnesses in the Gospel to one common Salvation, along with the British Churches, and how, in the new ecumenical instruments we are "no longer strangers, but pilgrims together in Christ*."*

I hope you have found joy in reading this account of the work of Christian Faith. I hope you will find a way of lending some support, somewhere, at some time. May God's grace and mercies abide with you always. Amen.

*See *The Swanwick Declaration* page 7, published by BCC, (See Appendix 1)

Appendix 1

SWANWICK DECLARATION*

The following 'Swanwick Declaration' was adopted by acclaim and personally signed by those present at The Hayes Conference Centre, Swanwick, on Friday 4 September 1987. The Conference asked that it should be read in Churches in England, Scotland and Wales on one of the Sundays in October.

No Longer Strangers -- Pilgrims!
Nid Diethriaid Mwyach -- Pererinion!
Luchd-Turuis -- Conhla!

Appointed by our Churches and under the guidance of the Holy Spirit we declare that this, the broadest assembly of British and Irish churches ever to meet in these islands has reached a common mind. We are aware that not all Christians are represented amongst us but we look forward to the time when they will share fully with us.

We came with different experiences and traditions, some with long ecumenical service, some for whom this was a new adventure. We are one band of pilgrims. We are old and young, women and men, black and white, lay and ordained, and we travelled from the four corners of these islands to meet at Swanwick in Derbyshire. There we met, we listened, we talked, we worshipped, we prayed, we sat in silence deeper than words. Against the background of so much suffering and sinfulness in our society we were reminded of our call to witness that God was in Christ reconciling the world to himself. We affirmed that this world with all its sin and splendour belongs to God. Young people called on us to be ready to sort out our priorities so that we could travel light and concentrate on our goal.

*The Swanwick Declaration is Chapter 3 of *Churches Together in Pilgrimage,* published for the Inter-Church Process ***Not Strangers but Pilgrims*** by the BCC.

Driven on by a Gospel imperative to seek unity that the world may believe, we rejoiced that we are pilgrims together and strangers no longer.

We now declare together our readiness to commit ourselves to each other under God. Our earnest desire is to become more fully, in his own time, the one Church of Christ, united in faith, communion, pastoral care and mission. Such unity is the gift of God. With gratitude we have truly experienced this gift, growing amongst us in these days. We affirm our openness to this growing unity in obedience to the Word of God, so that we may fully share, hold in common and offer to the world those gifts which we have received and still hold in separation. In the unity we seek we recognise that there will not be uniformity but legitimate diversity.

It is our conviction that, as a matter of policy at all levels and in all places, our churches must now move from co-operation to clear commitment to each, in search of the unity for which Christ prayed and in common evangelism and service of the world.

We urge church leaders and representatives to take all necessary steps to present, as soon as possible, to our church authorities, assemblies and congregations, the Report of this Conference together with developed proposals for ecumenical instruments to help the churches of these islands to move ahead together.

Continuing to trust in the promised gift of the Holy Spirit, we look forward with confidence to sharing with our own churches the joys of this historic Conference. We thank God for all those who, from Lent '86 and before, have been part of this pilgrimage. We feel their presence with us. We urge our churches to confirm by decision and action the hopes and vision on which we have laid hold, and which we shall not let go.

This is a new beginning. We set out on our further pilgrimage ready to take risks and determined not to be put off by 'dismal stories'. We resolve that no discouragement will make us once relent our avowed intent to be pilgrims together. Leaving behind painful memories and reaching out for what lies ahead,

We press on towards the full reconciliation in Christ of all things in heaven and on earth, that God has promised in his Kingdom.

Lord God, we thank you
For calling us into the company
Of those who trust in Christ
And seek to obey his will.
May your Spirit guide and strengthen us
In mission and service to your world;
For we are strangers no longer
But pilgrims together on the way to your Kingdom.
Amen.

Appendix 2

Extract from
THE ARCHBISHOP DAVID DOUGLAS'S ADDRESS TO THE CHURCHES
Delivered to the Nigerian Churches in 1995

UNITING THE CHURCHES

What is the meaning of coming together?
We become a force that is committed to achieve in all circumstances.

What is the reason for coming together?
We have conceded that working without consensus is a proven failure.

What are the objectives of being together?
To be a voice instead of voices: a voice that cannot be ignored.

What is the vision of being together?
It is a plan to succeed in carrying the message with power.

What are the requirements of being together?
Loyalty, integrity, peacefulness and love.

What is the commitment of being together?
We are committed to hard work, unity, unselfishness and caring.

What are the advantages of working together?
We are strengthened to uphold the truth.

What changes will be achieved by working together?
Power, authenticity, influence, support, independence.

Appendix 3

The Future

Although wonderful things have been accomplished, bringing so much good out of the struggles and suffering experienced by parents and grandparents, there is no doubt that there is much unhappiness, suffering, violence and personal inadequacy in our society and even worse situations in other parts of the world, especially those parts from which many of our Ministers and their people have come.

The world and its leaders are turning their attention to Africa. According to Thabo Mbeki, the President of South Africa, in his lecture "Perspectives on and of Africa", delivered at the Inaugural Lecture of the Parliamentary Millennium Project, "The 21st century (will) indeed be an African Century. ... Our struggle is to engage in both the total emancipation of our continent from the social, political and economic legacy of colonialism and apartheid, as well as to reclaim our history, identity and traditions, and on the foundation that our ancestors built for all humanity, rebuild our societies to ensure that they are developed and prosperous." As the world moves further along the process of globalisation, all of us need to be alert to influence that process to produce a world order that is just and peaceful.

Our Church bodies need to lead through government consultations and their specialist committees. We need to be able to operate at all levels, whether it is raising our own children in loving and well-ordered families, improving community life in every locality in the land in which we live, strengthening the Churches in other countries to do the same, or operating at national and international levels to bring about trade justice, an end to poverty and the responsible use and care of our planet.

To enable the next generation to bring to their neighbourhoods and to the world, to individuals and to communities, the benefits of the Gospel, IMCGB aims to continue to improve its provision of education for the Ministry and will seek to upgrade its colleges and add to their number. IMCGB will continue to equip its people to do good in the world, and in particular in the society in which they live. IMCGB is a movement which will bring something good in the future even though the world at present seems to be in a state of fluctuation and uncertainty.

We believe God will enable us to obey his command, **"Do not be overcome by evil, but overcome evil with good."*** **Romans 12:21.**

Rt. Rev. S. Douglas, May 2006

*See *The Holy Bible (NIV)*

Appendix 4

What is IMCGB?

IMCGB is a uniting body for Churches.
IMCGB sets standards for independent Churches.
IMCGB provides accountability, authenticity and recognition to Christian Ministers and their Churches through membership, licensing and ordination.
IMCGB empowers ethnic minority leadership, both men and women, and creates a forum to speak with one voice on issues such as immigration, asylum, racism, and social justice.
IMCGB provides ecumenical, theological and vocational training.
IMCGB has a leadership structure in the Bishopric, which offers care, guidance, counselling and representation of the Churches in wider society, ecumenical and government spheres.
IMCGB is regulated by the Office of Immigration Services Commissioner to provide immigration advice.
IMCGB works in many countries, encouraging Church projects, aiming to create a just and peaceful society through the Gospel.
IMCGB is financed by annual subscription, licence and ordination fees, donations and fundraising events.

How to join IMCGB

Apply by filling in the application form, obtained either by downloading from the website or by telephoning or visiting the IMCGB office.

The Church or Ministry and Leading Minister apply at the same time. Section A of the form is about the Church and section B about the Minister. Section B can be photocopied if more than one Minister is applying. The form must be accompanied by the Church's governing document, the Ministers' educational certificates, letters of recommendation, and fees.
The application will not be considered until all necessary documents and fees have been sent.

In United Kingdom there is a £300 joining fee and £60 ordination fee. Annual subscription worldwide is £100, annual licence fee £12.
The licensing committee meets 3 or 4 times a year.
Send applications to the IMCGB office in London.
If your country has an IMCGB Chapter,
send it to the office in your country.

Appendix 5

IMCGB Recognised Colleges

Bible Schools may apply to become IMCGB Recognised Colleges.

They must meet two criteria.

1.
IMCGB-recognised colleges will use materials produced by the International Correspondence Institute (ICI Global University) for preparation for the Ministry. Students of these colleges will complete the assignments laid down by ICI for assessment of their work. Assignments will be marked by the Adjunct Faculty member listed on the ICI website appropriate to the area in which a college is situated.

2.
In the United Kingdom colleges must meet Home Office requirements. In other countries they must qualify under the regulations of their government. The college must have an address at which lectures take place. Students must have adequate space and learning facilities such as library and computer access.

To obtain ICI materials, schools in the UK are invited to apply to our own ICI Learning Centre which runs in conjunction with
Immanuel Ministerial Training School.

Write to Rt. Rev. Onye Obika,
Community Resource Centre,
200 Langhedge Lane, London N18 2TJ.

You will be furnished with information about courses, modules, costs and accreditation and how to make a formal application.

Colleges in other countries, e.g.
Nigeria, Ghana, Kenya, India…,
should apply to the ICI Learning Centre in their country.

To apply to become an IMCGB-recognised college, write to the IMCGB Office in London
enclosing documentary evidence
that your school
meets the two criteria.

Appendix 6

(IMCGB)

ORGANISATIONAL CHART

MEMBER CHURCHES AND MINISTERS

PROJECTS AND COMMUNITY RESOURCE CENTRES

GENERAL PUBLIC

LOCAL GOVERNMENT

AGENCIES IN THE COMMUNITY

FAITH COMMUNITIES

TRUSTEES

SECRETARIAT
- INTERNATIONAL MODERATOR
- SECRETARY GENERAL
- ADMIN SUPPORT

COMMITTEES/DEPARTMENTS
- BISHOPS FORUM
- CO-ORDINATING FORUM
- OVERSEAS FORUM
- LICENSING FORUM
- IMMIGRATION FORUM
- CHARISMATIC IMPACT DEPARTMENT
- PROMOTION AND MEDIA FORUM
- UNITED CHURCH WELFARE AND WORKER'S ASSOCIATION (UCWWA)
- WATFORD RACE REPRESENTATIVE ORGANISATION (WRRO)

ANNUAL GENERAL MEETING
GENERAL MEETING

DEPARTMENT OF THEOLOGY AND LAW
ADJUDICATORS AND CHURCH LEADERS

ECUMENICAL REPRESENTATION
(CTBI, CTE, Racial Justice, Inter-Faith)
GOVERNMENT CONSULTATION

COMPLAINTS
INVESTIGATIONS
DISCIPLINE

MINISTERIAL TRAINING
PROFESSIONAL DEVELOPMENT
CONFERENCES
CONVENTIONS
ORDINATION SERVICES
YOUTH PROJECT
BEST PRACTICE IN UNITY
COUNSELLING AND ADVICE
WELFARE

153

INTERNATIONAL MINISTERIAL COUNCIL OF GREAT BRITAIN

FUNCTIONS OF COMMITTEES/DEPARTMENTS

BISHOPS FORUM
The work of Bishops, Statements to government and other agencies.

CO-ORDINATING FORUM
Co-ordinating events, Includes Publications, Newsletter.

OVERSEAS FORUM
Recruitment, Includes Education, IMCGB Approved Colleges, Overseas Chapters.

LICENSING FORUM
Ministerial Licensing, Church Registration.

IMMIGRATION FORUM
Immigration Advice. OISC regulated.

CHARISMATIC IMPACT DEPARTMENT
Prayer, Working Together, Research to inform debate, Fundraising, Media voice.

UNITED CHURCH WELFARE AND WORKERS' ASSOCIATION (IMCGB Social Services)
Support for Churches serving the community, Training, Advice, Grant Applications.

WATFORD RACE REPRESENTATIVE ORGANISATION (WRRO)
Community Relations Department, Racial Justice.

PROMOTION AND MEDIA FORUM

Appendix 7

IMCGB Personnel
as at November 2007

SECRETARIAT: Rt. Rev. S. Douglas, International Moderator
                Rt. Rev. O. Obika, Secretary General
TRUSTEES: Rt. Rev. S. Douglas,
          Rev. A. Baptiste,
          Rev. S. Wahab,
          Deacon S. Smith

                Members of the DEPARTMENT OF THEOLOGY AND LAW
BISHOPS' FORUM: Rt. Rev. S. Douglas, International Moderator
                      Rt. Rev. O. Obika, Secretary General
                      Rt. Rev. S. Addae, Moderator IMCGB Ghana Chapter
                      Rt. Rev. V. Mathew, Moderator IMCGB India Chapter
                      Rt. Rev. Lynette Melville, Shiloh United Church of Christ Apostolic
                      Rt. Rev. F. Akwaboah, Christian Hope Church
                      Rt. Rev. D. Thomas, WOW Ministries International
LICENSING AND DISCLOSURE FORUM: Rev. C. Ugwu, Chair
                                Rev. C. Brown, Secretary
                                Rev. E. Obika
                                Rev. A. Trethewy
                                Rev. M. Boston
IMMIGRATION FORUM: Rev. G. Assibey, Chair, Adviser
                        Rev. G. Sarfo-Duah, Adviser
                        Rev. E. Obika, Adviser
                        Rt. Rev. S. Douglas, Adviser
                        Rt. Rev. O. Obika, Supervisor, Adviser
CO-ORDINATING FORUM: Rt. Rev. D. Thomas, Chair
                           Rev. I. Owoyemi, Editor
                           Rev. N. Folson, Secretary
                           Rev. G. Muhoro
                           Rev. M. Owusu-Sekyere
                           Rev. A. Goretti

OVERSEAS FORUM: Rt. Rev. S. Douglas, International Moderator
Rt. Rev. O. Obika, Secretary General
Rt. Rev. S. Addae, Moderator Ghana Chapter
Rev. V. Mathew, Moderator Ghana Chapter
Rt. Rev. F. Akwaboah, Christian Hope Church
EDUCATION FORUM: Rt. Rev. S. Douglas, International Moderator
Rt. Rev. O. Obika, Secretary General
Rt. Rev. D. Thomas
CHARISMATIC IMPACT FORUM: Rev. G. Sarfo-Duah
Rev. G. Assibey
Rt. Rev. C. Maloney
Rev. Prince Daniels
Rev. Michael Adelasoye
Rev. Bridget Asuelime
Rev. A. Purchas
Rev. Sam-Best Ewruje
EDITORIAL BOARD: Rev. I. Owoyemi, Chief Editor
Rev. N. Folson
IMCGB CORE STAFF: Rt. Rev. S. Douglas, International Moderator
Rt. Rev. O. Obika, Secretary General

Appendix 8

Basis and Commitment of Churches Together in England (CTE)

Churches Together in England unites in pilgrimage those Churches in England which, acknowledging God's revelation in Christ, confess the Lord Jesus Christ as God and Saviour according to the Scriptures; and, in obedience to God's will and in the power of the Holy Spirit commit themselves:

to seek a deepening of their communion with Christ and with one another in the Church, which is his body, and

to fulfil their mission to proclaim the Gospel by common witness and service in the world, to the glory of God, Father, Son and Holy Spirit.

Churches Together in Britain and Ireland is now an agency of the Churches in the ecumenical instruments in the four nations, England, Scotland, Wales and Ireland.

Editor's Note:

David Douglas was a man of action, who researched to establish the problems and studied to find solutions. He suffered personally from the rejection and discrimination of racism and shed many tears on account of the struggles of black people. The church must lead in providing solutions and the Christian traditions and leadership styles that the immigrant black people brought with them to the UK must be recognised as authentic. At the same time, black Christian Ministers must be, and be seen to be, trained, licensed and accountable.

This book traces the founding of the International Ministerial Council of Great Britain (IMCGB), the Council that sets the standards for independent, charismatic Churches and their Ministers, from the disappointments and disillusionments of the immigrants of the late 1950s to the Inauguration of the first Pentecostal Archbishop selected and consecrated according to due process.

It also issues a challenge to civil authorities. David Douglas's foresight and resulting action did much to defuse the situation caused by racism in the 1960s, 70s and 80s. The book gives us some idea of how inner cities struggled with divisions and opposition caused by ignorance as well as lack of leadership and planning, resulting in great hardship, poor living conditions, inequalities in education, employment and housing, in a system which caused disadvantage to the African diaspora. The book is a warning to governments and all holding authority and power of leadership: have foresight, look ahead, plan to prevent situations which put a strain on our communities: bridge the gap between rich and poor and create a society that nurtures emotional, social, physical, moral and spiritual well being, instead of a dysfunctional system in which many are deprived in all these areas. Do not neglect to encourage the strong, rich, profound and necessary undergirding of communities by Christianity.

In editing this book I have edited out much of the author's comments on political figures, which detracted from the main theme of the founding and purpose of the IMCGB, and have concentrated on the thinking behind IMCGB, its philosophy and the relationship between the spiritual and social work of the Church.

Integral to David Douglas's strategy to lift black people out of their position in the lower strata of society and the experience of racial discrimination, was a special relationship of working together and sharing resources between white-led and black-led Churches. For this to be successful, Churches had to come into this partnership from a position of equal strength and equal esteem.

This book is about black people by a black man, telling how a black-led organisation was formed by means of which black people could provide for their own people as well as extending their ability to give to and appreciate esteemed members of white society. Only a black person can truly know what it is like to be black. Only a black person can tell it like it is. David Douglas did not see black people as an interesting research project. He carried them on his heart.

Rt. Rev. S. Douglas, 4th November 2007

INTERNATIONAL MINISTERIAL COUNCIL OF GREAT BRITAIN
DEPARTMENT OF IMMIGRATION

The IMCGB Department of Immigration is an advice service exempted by the Office of Immigration Services Commissioner (OISC).
Exemption number N200100481

This means that our advisers are permitted to give immigration advice and are trained and committed to standards required by the British government. We operate within the not-for-profit sector.

For further information, please call the IMCGB London Office or visit our website.

IMMANUEL MINISTERIAL TRAINING SCHOOL
An IMCGB-recognised college

Offers full-time and part-time Ministerial Training courses. Valid for Home Office visa.

For Prospectus and application form, please call or write to:
Community Resource Centre,
200 Langhedge Lane,
Edmonton, London N18 2TJ.

Telephone 020 8345 5169

THE HANDBOOK OF THE INTERNATIONAL MINISTERIAL COUNCIL OF GREAT BRITAIN
Third Edition

By David Douglas
Edited by S. M. Douglas

For a complete understanding of the vision, philosophy and practice of the Council
All members and those considering membership should read this handbook with their leadership teams.
Ecumenical partners and government agencies will find it helpful to understand the uniqueness of this vision.
Contains explanation of the Bishopric, Pentecostal liturgies, and a tribute to our Founder, Archbishop David Douglas.

ISBN 1 871757 053   IMCGB Publications   £5.00
(£5-50 by post)

IMCGB Head Office
217 Langhedge Lane, London N18 2 TG
Tel./fax: 020 8887 6468
Email: imcgb@aol.com web:www.imcgb.org

INTERNATIONAL MINISTERIAL COUNCIL OF GREAT BRITAIN

A UNITING BODY FOR CHURCHES